BRAND

Bruce I. Newman
DePaul University

Todd P. Newman
Stony Brook University

Kendall Hunt
publishing company

Cover Design created by Judith A. Newman

www.kendallhunt.com
Send all inquiries to:
4050 Westmark Drive
Dubuque, IA 52004-1840

This book is dedicated to Judith A. Newman and Erica L. Newman.

CONTENTS

ACKNOWLEDGMENTS

This book was truly a joint effort that we were able to accomplish through a very unique and special association between a father (Bruce) and son (Todd), both of whom are engaged in the scholarly pursuit of related, but different, fields of study. Bruce's work in marketing and political marketing, combined with Todd's work in science and environmental communication provided the axis from which the book was conceived. We realized that the role of branding is paramount in each of our respective disciplines, and as we investigated the best practices followed, it became clear that there was a much more important message that needed to be communicated when it comes to branding, and that was the overlap that existed across a wide range of brand entities, from a product, to service, to person, to organization, to nation, to an idea. Over the 2½-year period we were engaged with the project from the inception of the idea for the book through the research, analysis, synthesis, and writing up of the chapters, it was an eye-opening endeavor that we are very excited to share with you, the reader.

This book could not have been completed without the assistance, encouragement, and support of several different people. We want to thank all of the editorial staff at Kendall Hunt we worked with over a two-year period for their support, which includes Shannon Roney (Acquisitions Editor); Niki Price (Acquisitions Editor); Elizabeth Cray (Senior Project Coordinator); and Heather Richman (Graphic Designer). All of them were a delight to work with, and a special thanks goes to Elizabeth who worked very patiently with us as deadlines were delayed and reset, as well as to Heather, who used her creative talents to go back-and-forth with us to develop the final book cover design.

We want to identify all of the graduate assistants in the Kellstadt Graduate School of Business at DePaul University who worked very closely with us to carry out the extensive research that was necessary to develop the theoretical and strategic contributions of the book. These include Maria Upenskaya, Dale Crawford, and Emily Bourne. In particular, Emily worked extremely closely with us to help with the editing and writing during the final stages of the book. She was a tireless worker who deserves special mention. We also want to thank two of our colleagues at DePaul University, Professor Al Muniz and Professor Rich Rocco, both of whom were willing to read, critique, and offer invaluable suggestions on an earlier draft of the manuscript. In particular, Al was very helpful with his extensive comments and recommendations, and in particular, his insights on the role of brand communities, which reflects on his broad-based knowledge of the literature in this area.

Finally, we want to thank Judy Newman, Erica Newman, Alex Bleiweiss, Carol Watson, and Jack Watson, all of whom were very helpful with their ideas and feedback on various versions of the book cover. The origin of the idea behind the book cover came from Judy's sketches that were used by the artistic editorial staff to communicate the idea that virtually anything and anyone can be a brand.

Bruce I. Newman, PhD is a Professor in the Department of Marketing at DePaul University.

Todd P. Newman, PhD is a Postdoctoral Research Associate at the Alan Alda Center for Communicating Science at Stony Brook University.

CHAPTER 1

THE MEANING OF BRANDS

INTRODUCTION

For several years now, the Coca-Cola Corporation has relied on the sales of mainly one product to keep the company successful, namely the soft drink Coke. In fact, if there is one brand that is known around the world, it is Coke. But the company is beginning to realize that there is a certain risk to relying on a single product to define the brand of the company. In fact, the new CEO of Coke, Mr. James Quincey, is working hard to move the company beyond its core brand, Coca-Cola. In that effort, Mr. Quincey is trying to get his corporate staff to spend more time on research & development and innovation to go beyond their core base of soda, which brings in 70 percent of their global sales. This over-cautious strategic posture by a corporation, now 131 years old, that owns the most valuable brand in the world is the result of their previous failure in 1985 when the company decided to alter the taste of Coke and rename it "New! Coke." Mr. James Quincey, CEO, believes that Coca-Cola needs to become what he refers to as a "total beverage company." In his words, it means they cannot be afraid to take on new risk in their product development as well as with their relationship with bottlers in the distribution channel.[1]

Coca-Cola's brand situation is one that faces many companies when consumer tastes and demand changes, as is the case with the drinking habits of consumers who are not drinking as much soda. Even with the company's push into bottled waters and other beverages, the CEO thinks it is still possible to increase their share of the market in sodas with some product changes, like moving toward higher-margin products that

1

come in the form of smaller bottles at a higher price point. Beyond that, the company is also moving to increase its share of the market in energy drinks, tea, and coffee drinks, as well as sports drinks. It is also introducing into the market new products such as Fanta and Sprite with less sugar, as well as Coca-Cola Zero Sugar. So as simple as it might seem when it comes to marketing such a well-known brand as Coke, comes the difficulty of responding to changing consumer needs and wants, as well as to competition that is entering their market space with new and different soft drinks.[2]

On the other hand, take an example of a complex idea like climate change and consider what it would take to successfully brand this social issue in the minds of citizens in countries around the world. Just put your feet into the shoes of former Vice President Al Gore who is trying to work with strategists to develop a promotional campaign to make the case that climate change is an urgent problem and needs to be addressed. What is the best way for him to communicate a message on this subject, and would it be possible to develop a branding strategy in a similar way as one would for Coca-Cola? The difficulty in trying to explain climate change results from the deeply complex nature of the subject matter. By definition, it is a subject that has many different meanings to people and organizations who both support and refute the existence of it. This brings us to the dilemma of the strategist who is trying to develop a promotional campaign to drive a point of view on a complex subject matter, or for a politician for that matter, and raises a very important question: What is the best way to communicate a message about each of these examples, and are their commonalities across the branding strategy used for each one, or would each require a completely different branding campaign?

The answer to this hypothetical question is that whereas there may be some similarities in the development and execution of these branding campaigns, each would require very different strategies. First of all, climate change is a highly complex subject matter. It means different things to different people, and is debated about in a wide array of media channels. Furthermore, it is hard to pin down with images that define it. On the other hand, Coke is a very tangible product, easily identified by anyone, and can be communicated with pictures of the soda in a bottle or can. Unlike climate change, one single message can be used to convey the essence of the product, which is that as a soft drink. However, when it comes to marketing a politician, like Donald Trump, the branding strategy becomes more complicated, but in a different way than it is for climate change. Unlike climate change, there is no confusion about who Donald Trump is, but similar to the case of climate change, there is certainly a fair amount of confusion on what he stands for and whether or not he will be a good president. It is possible to draw out more similarities and differences between these examples, but suffice it say that each would require unique branding strategies.

This book will report on a comprehensive analysis of the different roles that brand plays across a wide range of entities, connecting both the common and unique aspects that branding plays in a manner that has never before been addressed. Marketers are all in the business of promising something to someone, and when it works successfully, the promise made is fulfilled with the delivery of a brand. People and organizations are constantly trying to figure out how best to brand themselves, their products, services, and ideas in a way that makes them competitive and stand out in the minds of their customers and various targeted audiences. At the same time, organizations and individuals selling their ideas to the general public, including professionals, political parties, and various nonprofits are oftentimes trying to convince a skeptical public about the changes taking place in society, and must rely on some of the same strategic principles to successfully market themselves.

In fact, brands are applied to everything, from museums to religions to universities.[3] This notion of having to rely on branding to communicate a succinct and clearly defined message even extends to nations that are in the business of swaying world public opinion.

So, one must ask the intuitive question, "What do all of these entities have in common, and how will branding strategies change as we move from corporation to nonprofit to political organization to nations?" This is what we seek to address in this book, with examples from different sectors of society, where organizations seek to drive the thinking of segments of people, some of who will be believers, and others who will not. We hope that it will shed a new light on the importance of taking a "cross-sector" approach to the understanding of one of the most basic principles we teach our students in marketing, which is the importance of understanding the needs and wants of customers before developing a product or service. Additionally, we hope this will provide valuable insights as to appropriately developing a promotional campaign aimed to educate and persuade others to respond positively to the agenda of the given organization.

As organizations in the for-profit, nonprofit, and political sectors in society work feverishly to keep up with the technology advances taking place in their respective markets, another question that arises is how this information be leveraged to market a more effective brand. Across the many different sectors that marketers work in, there is always one constant: The fundamental need to distill the meaning and value of their organization into an easily identifiable entity that effectively reaches and resonates with different segments of customers, citizens, and any other definable groups of people depending on what market the organization works in. In this book, we will seek to cut across the many different sectors where branding is a key tool used to enable an organization to accomplish their goals and stay competitive in their respective market. According to O'Guinn and Muniz, "Brands are created by interactions of multiple parties, institutions, publics, and social forces." They also make the point that a brand can also include bundles of meaning which allows it to be part of myth markets. Their work speaks to the myriad of voices and stakeholders that are often involved in the branding of many different entities.[4]

Positioning a brand in a clear, concise manner in the minds of a targeted audience allows an organization to separate its product, service, or whatever they may be marketing from the competition. The role of a brand thus becomes the key avenue through which companies can continue to reinforce the meaning attached to their offerings. Over time, the importance of maintaining one, clear meaning in peoples' minds is paramount, especially as organizations branch out into new markets, with new products and services. This goal has become increasingly more difficult as the digital age continues to move communication channels from the more traditional outlets like television, magazines and newspapers, etc., to the more high-tech channels that include social media and various Internet-related options like e-mail and others.

One of the key goals of branding is to bring about behavior change, but as it is well known in marketing circles, this usually must be preceded by changes in the way people think about a product, service, or any other entity. It is not sufficient just to educate people about a given product, service, person, organization, nation, or an idea, but it is imperative to persuade them before a change in behavior is possible. The argument we will put forward in this book is that brand is a multi-faceted construct that includes a wide range of meanings to different people in different sectors of society. Some have argued that information/cognition and emotion only tell part of the story about brands, especially when it comes to some areas like climate change, and that meaning plays a far larger role in the branding process.[5, 6]

In fact, a brand can also pertain to a nation, such as Russia, whose leader is seeking to define his country in the minds of people around the world. It is a deeply complex exercise from a marketing vantage point to arrive at a brand concept for Russia that will communicate the culture, values, and characteristics of the Russian people to others all around the world. Specifically, one has to begin to wonder how Vladimir Putin, the president of Russia, has used branding to elevate the status of his country from a second-tier nation, to one that has been at the center of controversies and debate that puts him and his country in the news on a regular basis.

We are excited to bring together in this book, for the first time, a careful examination of the branding of all entities, ranging from simple to complex, to outline how the branding process will differ across different sectors of society. We will also discuss the best practices in branding applicable to different examples supported by a thorough review of the academic literature in each of these areas and case studies of how organizations are actively engaged in the branding process.

A STRATEGIC BRAND FOCUS

We live in a time when it has become more difficult to control for the flow of information that is moving at lightning fast speed across the Internet with the new power that exists in social media. Considering this from a political perspective, in the past couple of years, we've observed dictators being taken down in the Arab Spring as a result of newly effective communication vehicles on social media, and a newly elected president in the United States who shocked the world with an unconventional victory built on the foundation of Twitter and Facebook. These events, influenced by the power of digital branding, are further evidence that all branding that occurs today across different categories have much in common that needs to be better understood. By exploring the common denominator across the different brand categories, it will become possible to arrive at a set of best practices that will be put forward in the last chapter of this book. However, before best practices can be determined, there needs to be a framework from which the interested party, be it a professional seeking to define his/her brand as they go from job-to-job in their career, marketing brand manager, climate change scientist, political operative, nonprofit manager, or even the leader of a nation, can better understand how to begin to evaluate the findings in the branding literature over the last several decades. With this in mind, we now turn to a framework (Figure 1.1) that will provide the basis from which to integrate the findings in the literature.

Whereas the technological advances that exist today will work to advance the thinking of all marketers, at the heart of a successful branding strategy is an understanding of the needs and wants of your customers, regardless of who that person might be.[7] In some cases, it might be a consumer in the commercial marketplace, or a citizen in the political marketplace. The focus of a branding strategy goes beyond the targeted audience, and must take into consideration who it is that is attempting to brand something

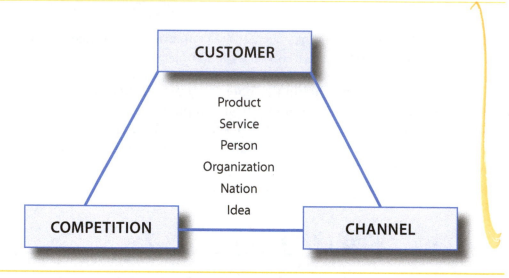

FIGURE 1.1   Strategic Brand Focus

or someone. Depending on who it is that is developing the branding strategy, the competition will vary, and it could be another similar organization within the same marketplace that one is operating in, or perhaps even one that operates across country borders.

Finally, when one looks beyond a targeted audience and the competitive market one is operating within, it is necessary to understand the channels through which a communications strategy would be carried out through. For example, the Tesla Corporation sells a very innovative product that has been branded as such, with high-tech features that take advantage of the use of electricity to power the automobile. The question that then arises is through which media channels should Tesla use to leverage its brand identity, and how should that decision be made in light of the customers they are targeting and with respect to their competition? The choice of channels, with a focus on communication outlets, but not limited to them, becomes an imperative for any organization in the business of branding. For example, during a political campaign, channels can include social media, traditional media (such as print, radio, and television ads), as well as a volunteer network, driven by e-mail and mobile phone application marketing. Hence, the definition of a channel for the more non-traditional entities covered in this book may include alternatives that one would not consider if the branding strategy centered on a simple product or idea, or even an individual who is trying to brand themselves, where a critically important channel could include person-to-person interaction.

In Figure 1.1, we pull together the 3 C's, which will include the Customer, Competition, and Channel. Each of these parts of the strategic brand focus will be explained, along with the integration of them into the six categories of brands that will be discussed in Chapters 2 through 7. This figure will serve to tie together the literature as it is discussed in each one of these chapters. For each of these brand categories, a part of each chapter will be devoted to synthesizing the literature along these lines of thinking, with the intent to move toward the identification of a set of best practices that one can follow in each of the 3 C's.

Customer

To begin with, any entity that seeks to brand their particular entity, whether it is a person, organization, or nation, must have an understanding of who their customer is and what it is that their targeted audience seeks from what is being branded. If we look at the automobile industry, whether a company is seeking to satisfy a customer's need for safety when it comes to buying a car, or another customer's need for innovation, corporations need to carry out research to determine whether they have the resources and ability to develop cars that can satisfy those customer needs.

For example, Volvo has historically sought to brand itself as a company that responds to the safety needs of consumers by developing their automobile brand as one that will instill a sense of security in those customers' minds, and backed up with features that reinforce that brand identity. Automobile features such as the body construction or even the use of air bags may serve to satisfy those needs. On the other hand, there are customers who seek the latest technological advances in cars, and may look to GM that developed the Volt, for a car that satisfies their needs for fuel efficiency. There have been several new cars marketed over the past several years that have brought in alternative fuel options for customers who don't want to pay premium prices for gas, so they seek out cars run on batteries and electricity. The needs of the customer base for these two very different products are recognized and capitalized upon in the branding strategies each company uses. Volvo's brand messaging aligns with its market positioning as a safety leader in the automobile industry, and communicates this throughout all marketing materials as a core competency of the company. However, GM's focus on those customers who are seeking a technologically advanced automobile would require a very different brand messaging, centered around performance, innovation, and novelty rather than a prominent focus on safety.

All organizations must engage in a process referred to as market segmentation, where the needs and wants identified in a marketplace are broken down to reflect the aggregated views of key market segments that hold the promise of a strong return on a company's resources if they focus their brand on the basis of a unique set of needs and wants. Every marketplace has key segments of customers, which in the automobile industry could be broken down at a very fundamental level for those customers seeking to buy a sedan, as opposed to a van, or an SUV. Further breakdowns in the automobile market exist, which include customers who buy on the basis of company loyalty, or resale value, or design and aesthetic features that are attractive. There is no end to the level at which a company can break down a market into segments, and this is the key point behind any branding strategy, and that is to determine which key segments exist, what their interests are, and whether it will serve as an attractive market to target from a financial point of view.

As we seek to extend the construct of branding beyond the traditional areas that have been studied in marketing, it is necessary to extend the focus beyond just the customer and include other roles that individuals play in society, such as in the role of a citizen. This is to say that as politicians, political organizations, nations, and climate change experts seek to brand their respective ideas, they are targeting citizens, not customers. Yes, one could argue that a citizen is by definition a customer, seeking to get benefits from government or other institutions that can have an impact on their life through the welfare of the environment for example, we choose to broaden the focus of branding to include citizens. This will become increasingly more important as disciplines such as political marketing help us to understand the intertwining of customer, voter, and citizen into a single person, who effectively play each of these different roles.

Competition

Along with an analysis of the needs and wants of the customer comes the realization that although a target market may exist that is interested in a branded product that has specific features that satisfies their needs, it may not be feasible for a company to develop such a product successfully if there are other companies who have greater resources, economies of scale, or sheer technological know-how that make it near impossible to market a brand that will succeed in a highly competitive marketplace.

This raises the importance of positioning a brand in a crowded market so that it stands out as an option that has a competitive advantage over other brands in the market. Competitive advantage derived from differentiation is precisely how brands evolve and survive to meet the ever-changing needs and preferences of the consumer. For example, in the hand soap market, bars were the sole alternative for many years until the concept of soft soap came into existence. The unique position of soft soap was the user-friendly use of this form of soap, and offered new benefits for some of its key segments. The hotel industry in particular found this differentiated product particularly appealing, as soft soap was resource efficient. Hotels no longer had to throw away bars of soap after only one or two uses; instead, the soft soap, which was filled into a container, could be easily refilled, still look new, and complied with sanitary requirements. Every branded product needs to stand out from the competition, and a deep understanding of target market needs should drive brand differentiation strategies.

The same argument that exists across competitors does so across nations. The brand of a political leader shapes the perceived brand of the country. One could argue that Xi Jinping of China is facing a similar branding challenge as any organization that is attempting to define its products in the minds of its customers. The perception of the Chinese brand is very much affected by geo-political efforts on the part of countries who seek to both befriend and oppose China on the grounds of political actions that China has taken that has impacted the safety and security of other nations. Certainly, one could look at the efforts of the Trump administration, representing the U.S. as a competitive force that is working to cooperate with China, and effectively strengthen the brand of Mr. Xi in an effort to work with him to neutralize the threat of North Korea. Using branding at the nation-level of course coincides with the definition of a citizen, rather than a customer, whose attention and support is sought by leaders. Nevertheless, brand strategy and differentiation heavily influences an entire nation's political climate, and highlights the importance of effectively implementing core branding concepts.

We live in an age where politics is played out instantaneously between leaders and nations on the Internet in a digital format, and without an understanding of the increasingly more important role that political communication is taking in a global environment, nations will be hard-pressed to stay competitive. The case of politics will be made throughout the book, and represents a very interesting example of how the branding of leaders can be unique in many ways, as will be detailed in later chapters, but also represents the application of best practices to other entities in different sectors where there is a similar complexity to the branding challenge.[8]

Channel

This brings us to the third C, namely the channel that is used to implement a successful branding strategy. This of course ties into the unique characteristics of the entity seeking to carry out the branding strategy that makes it possible to leverage its strengths and experiences as it relates to the brand in question. For example, the people and organizations that are involved in the sustainability movement in the U.S. will rely more or less heavily on very different channels to communicate to their customers (or interested citizens) to impact their thinking and actions on the subject. Coca-Cola, on the other hand, which relies on channels like television, events, print, and social media to reach its customer base will not put the same reliance on channels such as demonstrations, corporate sponsorships, partnerships with governments and public-sector agencies, or even speeches by influential opinion leaders who are in the business of branding climate change. The same logic holds true for political organizations seeking to sell their candidate to an electorate, who will rely more on a volunteer network, in addition to the other more traditional channels of communication, as they seek to get out the vote on Election Day.

As this part of Figure 1.1 is discussed, it is important to get an understanding of the organization or entity that is involved in the branding process, and to take into account their capability to carry off the branding strategy successfully. Whereas all companies that seek to satisfy the needs of their customers operate on the principle that they must be in a position to develop the research and development (R&D) processes to manufacture products that meet the needs of their customers, the actual ability to execute this may be very difficult. For example, take the case of Apple, a company that essentially created the mobile phone market. Through the sheer technological strength of their R&D department, they were able to manufacture the revolutionary iPhone which to this day continues to be a top smartphone provider globally. One would have to raise the rhetorical question, "So why didn't other companies jump into the market with phones that were developed with similar features as the iPhone?"

The answer lies in the fact that the core competency of other companies in this industry was not capable of producing a brand with identical features. Apple's brand since the company's inception has been sleek, innovative, and futuristic, so naturally their first-to-market approach and buzz generated by the iPhone launch could not be replicated. Even if another company had created an identical design, the branding of Apple as a company is what made the iPhone a superior product in the consumers' minds at the time. However, Samsung accurately adapted to this new competition by developing the first Android phone utilizing advances put forward by Google. In summary, Samsung created and effectively leveraged its Google partnership as a core competency and key differentiating factor from Apple. Similar to Samsung's inability to compete with Apple's first-to-market strategy, Apple cannot compete with the technological and customizability features Samsung offers. As a result, these products compete with different segments of the smartphone customer, and each brand capitalizes on its core competencies to sell iterations of their smartphones. Samsung and Apple effectively created different brand-loyal segments of customers based on their unique core competencies, fueling their current and future successes in the marketplace. To this day, there are diehard Apple fans and diehard Android fans, cultivated by successful branding of each product by each company. All organizations must be involved in this kind of strategic analysis if they expect their brands to be successful in their respective marketplaces. Without a strategic brand focus, it becomes impossible for any organization, or a person for that matter, to be successful in their branding initiatives.

WHAT IS A BRAND?

A brand is defined as the essence of a product, service, idea, person, organization, or nation that conveys meaning on multiple levels to different segments of people. Branding involves the process of creating a name, image, and logo that distinguishes and separates an entity from competitors that defines it and makes it possible for it to stand out as unique and different in the minds of people. A powerful brand strategy gives you a noteworthy edge in increasingly aggressive markets. Essentially, a brand is the culmination of your promise to your client. It lets them know what they can expect from you, what value you bring, and how others perceive you.

The role of branding is becoming increasingly important today, and in a rapidly evolving digital world saturated with social media, news outlets, and interactive engagement, new marketing channels are shifting the way brands interact with their audiences. This is further complicated by the movement toward online distribution channels that don't afford a company the opportunity to connect with their customer in a face-to-face situation. Along with staying current on the ever-evolving digital landscape, brands must continuously innovate to reach and build strong connections with their audiences. The traditional face-to-face interaction between brand and consumer is rapidly declining, if not already obsolete, and thus it is imperative for brands to correctly navigate this to stay competitive.

A brand strategy is the way in which an organization plans on communicating their brand message to a desired audience. Brand strategy encompasses the channels through which the brand is communicated. By relying on a consistent, clear, and unique branding strategy, it becomes possible for a company to build up its brand equity, which refers to the additional value the audience connects to an organization's products or services. Strong brand equity is a powerful tool to further differentiate from competitors, and can be a critical factor in the customer's ultimate decision when comparing two similar brands.[9]

Product branding is a concept that is used in both the Business-to-Consumer and Business-to-Business sectors. Whereas there has been a shift from products to services, in what one could refer to as the "age of services," there is still a significant amount of attention to the branding of products. For those companies in the business of branding a product, they must determine what exactly is required to create a strong brand, and then translate those needs into an action plan, or brand strategy. A common branding challenge many companies face is how to determine the appropriate way to integrate two or more parent brands that start playing the roles of a "host" and an "ingredient."[10] Researchers have been trying to determine what effect this has on the parent brand, especially when it comes to a product failure in the marketplace.

WHY IS BRANDING IMPORTANT?

The phenomenon of branding is omnipresent in our culture: We can observe and interact with brands on a daily basis, from glimpsing at a billboard during our morning commute to reading a news article detailing current events around the world, to engaging in a conversation with a doctor about a medicine he or she recommends. One could argue that the strongest brands are those that elicit some type of emotion from their audiences. Consider this from a consumer perspective: We describe our favorite brands based on how they resonate with us as consumers, so when we say, "trademarked product" or "excellent service," or "favorite hotel," we are communicating that we relate on a deeper level to a brand, and it evokes a feeling we use to communicate to others. Yet, there are others who have argued that the strongest brands are those that speak to cultural contradictions and disruptions.[11, 12] For example, consumers sometimes like to see a brand as a way to resolve a certain contradiction or tension that exists within them, whether it is voting for (or against) a presidential candidate who represents a certain set of core values, or not purchasing products from companies whose philosophy one does not agree with.

Brands aim to reassure us that the product or service we buy is authentic, and that it will deliver on the promises marketed to us. Customers aim to find the optimal balance of price and perceived benefits for their unique needs. Given the ever-present level of connectivity we operate in today, customers are aware of almost all of the possible options just by looking at the screens of their smartphones. As a result, companies strive to communicate their unique selling point (USP) more than ever.[13] Capitalizing on authenticity in order to build trust with customers is arguably more important now than it ever has been given the nearly unlimited access the customer has to conduct research, compare prices, and gather candid feedback and reviews from other customers.

BRAND CONCEPT MANAGEMENT

Park, Jaworski, and MacInnis introduced a framework for selecting, implementing, and managing brand image.[14] According to their research, oftentimes the brand image is managed based on the current analysis of the competition and brand performance. However, the authors emphasized that this approach is neither strategic nor holistic. Rather, brands need to adhere to their unique positions within the framework they identify to devise a differentiated but concise brand image. The framework can help brand managers through the initial brand concept before market entry to the subsequent three-stage process: introduction, elaboration, and fortification.

The framework proposed by Park et al. includes the three facets:

1. Communication of brand image
2. Operating activities (product availability, accessibility, consumer's willingness to overcome barriers)
3. Marketing mix elements consistent with the above points

The authors emphasized the importance of consistency in brand positioning and brand differentiation in managing a strong brand image over time. Their research states that the pre-market brand concept should be built on consumer needs, and can either be functional (intended to solve a specific problem), symbolic (intended to tie into the ego of the individual), or experiential (which would tie into a sensory-oriented dimension). According to the authors, symbolic needs and consumption are intertwined. Symbolic meaning is created when the consumer associates the product or service with a desired group, role, or self-image. The study indicates that positioning a product in all of the three categories is possible, but its management will be extremely difficult because a product branded in this fashion will face a higher risk of miscommunication, inconsistency, and competition. Research in this area has also been carried out from a sociological perspective.[15, 16, 17]

BRANDING AS A RELATIONSHIP

Customers understand that distinct characteristics and experiences affect their perception of a brand. So, the question arises as to why customers choose one brand over another. Why are some people thrilled to learn about the biography of a certain celebrity or a successful business person? Why are some customers interested in buying a product when they don't really need it, like a new blouse or fancy piece of jewelry? The answer is that brands help us develop our own self-identity, as well as how we are perceived by others.

Rooney emphasized the ability of people to relate to inanimate objects and form meaningful bonds with them on the basis of their emotional appeal, pointing out the significance of not relying on objective-oriented dimensions of a brand to communicate with the customer.[18] Since branding is emotional and highly personal, different individuals can evaluate marketing campaigns and branding efforts in different ways. Hamann, Williams, and Omar explored differences in product perception.[19] Since branding is relational, sometimes customers may have certain unexpected brand associations that can be detrimental for the success of a branding campaign.[20] For example, take the Tesla automobile, which operates on the basis of electricity. With reports indicating that this could lead to the automobile being stranded on the side of the road, some potential customers are taking a second look at the Tesla, and taking into consideration this unexpected event that could shape their decision to go with this brand. There is a broad base of research in the consumer behavior literature that also speaks to the importance of the role of relationship in branding.[21, 22]

According to Gobe, the modern economy is focused on the consumer, and with the power of the Internet, modern branding involves an interactive dialog with the consumer.[23] Modern products not only can be experienced as physical objects or services, but also have a lot of intangible characteristics, often subjective and highly personal. To address the challenge of building customer loyalty in the cluttered information space, brand managers must devote their efforts to understanding the customer and meeting their needs.

Successful brand managers know that unmet needs are what drives the customer, and strong brands give customers a promise to "close the gap" in the pursuit of wholeness.[24] According to Wright, strong brands are created with a desire to improve the lives of customers and engage them in a meaningful dialog. Moreover, Wright concluded that completion, regulation, and self-actualization are the roles that brands may take on for their customers. Brands transcend the tangibility of benefits, hence the strong psychological attachments consumers have for brands on an unconscious level. Calder and Cook agree that the choice of a brand is highly emotional and lies in the needs of the customer.[25] However, the customer will rationalize this deepest bond when asked why he/she chooses the particular brand. This strong relationship, at times unbeknownst to the consumer, can be made with little consideration as a result of a strong emotional connection consumers attach to a brand, reinforcing the importance of understanding the emotional motivation that drives consumer behaviors.

Contrary to the common belief, persuasion in brand communication does not come first, but rather empathy.[26] According to Wright, empathy is one of the most crucial factors that produce brand loyalty. Empathy facilitates communication and makes the customer feel good about the product. When consumers develop positive feelings and associations about a product, they are more likely to engage in repeat purchasing behavior.

WHAT MAKES A BRAND IRRESISTIBLE?

Wright makes the point that the most important role of a brand is to give customers a certain level of comfort. According to his thinking, positive emotions are triggered by the visual identity of a brand, and products that improve our lives through a positive emotional connection helps to create more loyalty toward the company that sells it. The author argues that brands make us feel better by adding something in our lives that is missing, thus making us feel more whole as a person. Calder and Cook explored the characteristics that make brands irresistible. Irresistible brands appeal both to emotions, as well as to the rational decision-making process.[27]

For example, Apple customers are willing to stand in long lines to buy recently released products as they enter the marketplace. This notion of irresistibility effectively lowers a customer's price sensitivity. Calder and Cook argue that "irresistibility" is created when companies understand deep needs of the consumer and provide a product or service that will be consistently meeting the need, even in the case of a market crisis and/or societal transformations. An irresistible brand has to deliver the consistency and convey the desire to stay true to the customer and put his/her needs first.

Calder and Cook identified that for a brand to be irresistible it should meet eight main criteria:

- ▶ Be a know-how,
- ▶ Keep evolving,
- ▶ Convey meaning,
- ▶ Resonate with emotions,
- ▶ Stand out by using meaningful symbols,
- ▶ Connect well across function, emotions, and social actions,
- ▶ Provide seamless brand experience across multiple touchpoints,
- ▶ Stay consistent across categories.

Today, brand managers must effectively navigate an incredibly dynamic and challenging marketplace. The modern market is full of similar product offerings and lack of strong differentiation. Given the conditions, a company's success is contingent upon understanding what drives customer behavior, which needs are most important for the customer, and how to create a brand that capitalizes on these needs and projected behaviors.[28]

BRAND LOVE

Brand loyalty has always been paramount for scholars and marketing professionals. Previous studies indicate that the phenomenon of brand love is a possible antecedent of brand loyalty.[29, 30]

According to Park et al., exclusivity is an important element of brand love.[31] Undoubtedly, brand love can change the direction of modern brand management. Sternberg believes that love is related to liking, but it is not the same category.[32] Ultimately, the brand loyalty that is produced by brand love is much more powerful than the simple liking of a brand. According to the authors, brand love is founded on brand identification and the sense of community.[33] The authors supported the ideas of Belk and Fournier as the works had recognized that brand identification and a sense of community as antecedents of brand loyalty and brand love.[34, 35, 36]

Belk points out that things people possess can become part of their self-concept. His work developed the notion that consumption plays a key role in how consumers create their sense of identity, and this extends to the idea that people can be in love with their material possessions. Belk explains that a person's self-identity has multiple meanings, and beyond special possessions (such as a favorite watch or piece of jewelry), can include a person's lifestyle, hobbies, family, occupation and other aspects of their existence. Fournier's research established that a consumer may actually have a passionate emotional attachment to particular brands. Her work determined that a satisfied consumer's love is greater for brands in categories that are perceived to be more hedonic as opposed to utilitarian, as well as for brands that offer the consumer symbolic value. When this takes place, this higher level of brand loyalty can result in more positive word of mouth.

Bergkvist and Bech-Larsen suggested that brand managers should cultivate a sense of community through influencers and/or sponsorships.[37] Moreover, the authors emphasize that brands that provide sense of community and self-enhancement are likely to produce brand love. According to Park et al., brand lifestyles are an effective way to strengthen brand community and brand identification.[38] Brand love as a new marketing concept is not only recognized by scholars but also praised by marketing and advertising practitioners.[39]

INDUSTRIAL BRANDING

While a lot of attention has been given to branding of consumer products, business-to-business (B2B) branding has been understudied. However, modern organizations in the B2B industry do require effective branding to grow and effectively handle the competition. As Keränen, Piirainen, and Salminen emphasized, the consumer branding frameworks cannot be used for B2B branding without the ability to adjust when necessary and remain flexible.

B2B, or industrial branding, is an area where branding faces a lot of bias from managers and lack of attention and empirical data from scholars. Often, B2B brand managers apply the same principles that managers apply for consumer goods.[40] However, the following efforts lose their effectiveness, since B2B industry significantly differs from the B2C (business-to-consumer) market. As the authors highlight, B2B branding should take into consideration longer-term client relationships, higher number of decision-makers, and different communication channels. Moreover, service branding is also crucial for B2B companies that increasingly become "total solutions providers." Mudambi, Doyle, and Wong emphasized that credibility, strong corporate culture, and social responsibility are becoming crucial for industrial products as a main point of differentiation among commoditized offerings.[41]

INTRODUCTION OF NEW BRANDS AND CO-BRANDING

Many scholars highlight that effectively managed brand portfolios help drive a company's growth. As emphasized by Aaker, brands should not be viewed individually, but rather as a part of a brand system.[42] Brand architecture and carefully managed brand portfolios can be used to effectively segment and differentiate products in relationship to the competition. In fact, many companies unite their branding efforts to succeed in a highly competitive marketplace. In the modern marketplace, co-branding initiatives are often used as a more secure and economical way to introduce new products given high failure rates for new brands, which tend to hover around 80 to 90 percent.[43]

Besharat and Langan have conducted significant research on the topic of co-branding.[44] A co-brand is defined as the placement of two brand names on a new or improved product. According to the authors, co-branding is an effective strategy that helps reduce the cost of entrance into new markets. Along with the benefit of entering a market with a well-known and respected brand identity, companies are in a position to leverage that with reduced promotional costs due to the fact that customers are already familiar with the brand family, and do not need to be made aware of it, an expense that can be eliminated. The authors recommend managers treat individual brands as significant parts of the brand portfolio in order to properly assess and leverage brands while supporting the total structure of the brand portfolio.

According to Kotler and Armstrong, co-branding can be used for both new and improved products.[45] Co-branding efforts, according to Besharat and Langan, can help the companies enter a new market, improve product or service, or enhance brand image.

It is important to highlight that not all brand partnerships can be identified as co-branding. Besharat and Langan emphasized that the primary characteristics of genuine co-branding include:

- ▶ Long-term nature of the relationship,
- ▶ Integration of the logos of partnering companies on the package,
- ▶ Complementarity with the partnering brands retaining their independent nature and legacy at the same time.

According to the authors, successful co-branding is possible with the healthy integration of three components: two partnering brands and the consumer. Each of the constituencies exchange value. Based on the view of a value exchange framework introduced by Besharat and Langan, if partnering companies and the consumer do not have aligned goals and offer a weak value proposition, the co-branding initiative is likely to fail. Thus, it is imperative to critically analyze each brand's primary characteristics, and from there, determine which brands are best suited for co-branding.

Umbrella branding is another effective branding tactic used for new product introductions and the development of the brand. The term "umbrella branding" or "family branding" implies that the same brand name is used to name several products. According to Wernerfelt, the connection in umbrella branding acts as a "signal" that helps introduce a new product by transferring associations from the old product.[46] The method proved to be effective for the expansion of the existing brands, whether consumer goods or services such as restaurants, hotels, grocery stores, etc.

For those organizations that have developed a single, well-known, and well-respected brand in a market, where the product itself as opposed as the organization's reputation is what is driving the reputation of the brand, a co-branding strategy would be a better choice than an umbrella brand strategy. The opposite is true for the use of an umbrella branding strategy, where it is the organization that has developed several successful brands under the "banner" of the company's name. For example, if one were interested in purchasing a tool to use at home, Sear's development of the "Craftsman" line of tools sold at all Sears stores (that is up until the line of tools was sold to Stanley Black & Decker) would be in a better position strategically to rely on an umbrella branding strategy, where the name "Craftsman" carries with it a reputation for quality and durability. One could also argue that Unilever's "Axe" brand would be another example of the use of an umbrella branding strategy where similar products, such as deodorants and shower gels, are all sold under the same family brand name. On the other hand, a co-branding strategy would make more sense for a company like Red Bull that doesn't only sell energy drinks, but also other products not necessarily related directly to a drink, but products that tie into a particular lifestyle that connects them on the basis with some extreme level of activity.

GLOBALIZATION AND BRANDING

In the era of globalization, many researchers are trying to understand the branding frameworks behind foreign brands and domestic brands that build their brand equity on the perception of being a foreign product. Anholt examined how branding can sustain economic development of countries and help businesses grow and thrive.[47] Leclerc, Schmitt, & Dubé examined the effects of foreign branding on customer perception of a product.[48] According to their research, brand name and its pronunciation and spelling can significantly affect the consumer's perceptions of the brand. In the case of brands with foreign names, the customer often forms associations of the brand based on the perception of a particular country as a whole, rather than the product itself. For example, Haagen-Dazs ice cream is a product that is produced in Brooklyn, New York, in the United States, but has a perception of a European brand because of the spelling of the brand name. For those customers who accrue a more positive image to those products manufactured outside the U.S., this would affect their perception in a positive way.

Differentiation is a critical component for successful branding, whether of domestic or foreign products. Han and Terpstra examined the effects of country-of-origin and perceptual connections of brands and brand name on consumer evaluations of uni-national and bi-national products.[49] As the authors discovered, both the country of origin and the brand name significantly influence the perception of the quality of a product, with the country of origin having the most powerful effect on the perception. For example, the perception of automobiles such as a Mercedes or BMW is premised on the fact that German engineering offers a superior level of quality in the manufacturing of their automobiles. So, the connection of the country-of-origin of these automobiles provides a key factor for consumers to use as they evaluate them. Their findings support the importance of brand image and brand associations that should be created and effectively managed in the very competitive global marketplace that most companies operate within today.

CONCLUSION

Branding is an incredibly complex process, and extends past its traditional role as simply part of a marketing strategy. Traditionally defined as the process of creating a name, image, logo, and differentiating message that establishes an identity in relation to a good or service, branding is no longer just a set of marketing tactics. Rather, branding is a key component in any business's strategy; moreover, branding transcends it's traditionally thought of use as exclusively a business issue. Instead, branding encompasses the communication of a set of values as it relates to the public's perception of the brand entity in question, and is relevant to all businesses, including nonprofit and service based firms. Essentially, anything can (and should) be branded as a form of establishing and maintaining a narrative one wishes the general public to hold about your business, good, service, country, political candidate, etc.

Effective branding requires effective communication channels, meaning whatever product, service, or idea you are selling must resonate well with your targeted audience. It is imperative for consumers to absorb and understand your brand or message so that they can begin to appreciate and form their own perceptions of your brand in a way that aligns with how you want your audience to feel about your brand. Therefore, establishing a relationship with consumers drives brand success. A critical component of relationship building involves emotion. Brands that effectively elicit appropriate emotional responses from their targeted audiences are the most successful in establishing favorable brand perception, and ultimately brand loyalty. A brand's ability to relate to its audience is a powerful tool that ultimately drives purchasing behavior for goods and services, and garners support for more abstract entities like ideas, people, or places.

There are a variety of branding strategies at a marketer's disposal—most commonly, we see the attempt to establish brand love as a strategy, co-branding as a strategy, and umbrella branding. Brand love is a phenomenon closely related to driving emotion in consumers. Brand love aims to establish loyalty and brand champions through establishing such a strong connection to its consumer, above and beyond holding favorable perceptions of a brand. Instead, brand love creates brand advocates and seeks to grow its base of intense brand supporters to create a community of strong advocates. Co-branding is the process in which two brands are combined in such a way that the multiple brands are presented as a single identity, but combines key components of each individual brand. Co-branding is a tricky strategy that requires in-depth analysis of consumer perceptions to accurately identify which components of each brand are most favorable, and how to highlight each individual brand's strength without overshadowing the brand partnership by having a single dominant brand. Umbrella branding carries the same principles as co-branding, in which more than two brands are combined to create a single, uniform message across brands, and incorporates the same challenges and benefits as co-branding.

In an increasingly connected, Internet-dependent, and real-time expectant world, branding in the digital space has created new frontiers and ways in which consumers and brands interact. A key component of digitization is the power of the consumer voice, and an unprecedented call for user generated branding. Social media in particular is a driving factor that forces brand experts to take into account (and even encourage) consumer feedback that shapes brand perceptions and fuels brand strategy, development, and values.

Social media provides the opportunity for anyone and everyone with access to the channel to share thoughts, opinions, experiences, and personal stories about a brand. Because this information can be easily viewed, shared, or added to, the power of word of mouth is exponentially more influential on social media. Consumer expectations are elevated in today's digital environment, so much so that consumers expect to be able to get all questions answered, research a product, and easily understand authentic consumer experiences to consider before making a purchase. It is therefore a crucial piece of any brand to not only have a social media presence, but an effective one at that. Brands can interact with consumers for customer service questions or requests, as well as establish goodwill and favorable perceptions simply by being on these channels and taking the time and effort to reach consumers online in a way that is convenient and useful for them.

The role of branding is rapidly shifting, and is becoming increasingly more important and integral to the strategic planning process. Effectively articulating, communicating, executing, and maintaining a unified, powerful, and relevant message for any given brand is no easy feat, although the in-depth analysis and application of research explored in this book will provide valuable insights as to effective methods to approach and develop a branding strategy.

PLAN OF THE BOOK

In order to establish the inter-connectedness between branding in different sectors of society, and to highlight the unique tactical and strategic issues that need to be considered when branding across a broad spectrum of entities, the book will be divided into chapters that separate brand entities into six different categories. Chapters will be divided into "Brand Categories" that represent a natural breakdown across different sectors in society. The cross-sector approach this book takes represents the major theoretical and strategic contribution of the book, which is the fact that organizations in different sectors of society must be open-minded to the best practices that are followed not only in their respective markets, but in markets that may have no apparent overlap in theory, but much in practice.

In this book, we will attempt to point out how there is strategic and/or tactical overlap between brand entities that vary in scope, size, industry, and nature to help identify branding strategy from a cross-disciplinary basis. As the cross-disciplinary comparisons are made, it will become clear that there is a continuum on which brand categories can be compared that tie into the level of complexity of the category. The book will move from the more simplistic and traditional categories, like the branding of products, to services to organizations, to the more complex and nontraditional categories, like the branding of people, to political parties to nations to ideas. As this transition is made across chapters, the branding uniqueness and distinctions will be made with reference to companies in these different categories, and how each has successfully used branding in their respective marketplace. Ultimately, this analysis will lead to a concluding chapter that puts forward the best practices that exist across these categories, and a set of recommended strategies to follow depending on the brand in question. It is our intent to offer new insights on branding that takes advantage of the literature that exists in each of these areas, and to highlight the overlap between them, and to point out how executives in organizations across all categories, as well as individuals pursuing their own careers, can learn from one another to develop more successful branding strategies.

Chapter 2, The Branding of Products, will be devoted to a discussion of the more traditional literature that has reported on how products in both the for-profit and nonprofit sectors are branded.

Chapter 3, The Branding of Services, continues to explore a discussion of more traditional literature that moves the discussion of products to a slightly more complicated branding scenario, where there is not a tangible good to base a branding strategy on, as well as the fact that there exists the unpredictability of the operation of a service which comes with the human factor that plays a role in the delivery of services.

Chapter 4, The Branding of People, explores a wide range of individuals who use branding, both at an individual level and organizational level (for example, the use of celebrities as part of a marketing strategy). It will also cover the branding of politicians who use many of the same strategies as celebrities or individuals do, but in a different context, namely the political arena. Perhaps most importantly, the application of the tactical and strategic insights will be applicable to all professionals who seek to succeed in their careers with their own personal brand.

Chapter 5, The Branding of Organizations, will analyze how organizations across a wide spectrum of businesses use branding, whether it is for products and services that are bought on a daily basis, or for political organizations that use branding to market their candidate to the electorate. The extension to the branding a company will be taken one step further with a discussion of the branding nonprofit organizations.

Chapter 6, The Branding of Nations, represents an even more complex situation, where there are many different types of people and organizations that operate within a country who need to act in a coordinated effort to be successful. There is also the added level of complexity that comes with the competitive environment where other nations, and their leaders, may each have different agendas that presents varying levels of pressure and unpredictability, making this level of branding even more difficult to operate within.

Chapter 7, The Branding of Ideas, will cover social issues that represent complex ideas and advocacy where divergent groups of people and organizations seek to brand their respective arguments, such as one would find in the areas of climate change, sustainability, and genetically modified foods. Unlike a nation, where more tangible forms of identification with the source of the brand can be identified, as exists with a leader, this level of branding represents an even more challenging pursuit due to the broad cross-section of people and organizations who are advocating different points of view on the subject.

Chapter 8, Best Practices, will summarize the best practices that are currently used in each of the brand categories analyzed in the book, and make recommendations for people and organizations to follow to succeed at their branding strategies in the future.

Endnotes

1. Maloney, Shaking the 'New Coke Syndrome', 2017.
2. Maloney, Coca-Cola Needs to Be More Than Just Coke, Its Next Chief Says, 2017.
3. Muñiz Jr., 2015.
4. O'Guinn and Muñiz Jr., 2010.
5. Twitchell, 2004.
6. Fournier, Quelch and Reitveld, To Get More out of Social Media, Think Like an Anthropologist, 2016.
7. Newman, 2016.

8. Perloff, 2018.
9. STAFF n.d.
10. Radighieri, J.P., et al., 2014.
11. D. B. Holt, How brands become icons: The principles of cultural branding, 2004.
12. D. B. Holt, What becomes an icon most? 2003.
13. Hamann, Williams and Omar, 2007.
14. Park, Jaworski and MacInnis, 1986.
15. Berthon, et al., 2007.
16. Fournier, Solomon and Englis, When brands resonate, 2008.
17. Gyrd-Jones and Kornum, 2013.
18. Rooney, 1995.
19. Hamann, et al., 2007.
20. Hamlin and Wilson, 2004.
21. Fournier, Consumers and their brands: Developing relationship theory in consumer research, 1998.
22. Fournier, Exploring Brand-Person Relationships: Three Life Histories, 1997.
23. Gobe, 2009.
24. Wright, 2014.
25. Calder and Cook, 2014.
26. Wright, 2014.
27. Calder and Cook, 2014.
28. Hamann, et al., 2007.
29. Carroll and Ahuvia, 2006.
30. Batra, Ahuvia and Bagozzi, 2012.
31. Park, et al., 1986.
32. Sternberg, 1987.
33. Bergkvist and Bech-Larsen, 2010.
34. Belk, 1988.
35. Fournier, Consumers and their brands: Developing relationship theory in consumer research, 1998.
36. Fournier, Exploring Brand-Person Relationships: Three Life Histories, 1997.
37. Bergkvist and Bech-Larsen, 2010.
38. Park, et al., 1986.
39. Bergkvist and Bech-Larsen, 2010.
40. Keränen, Piirainen and Salminen, 2012.
41. Mudambi, Doyle and Wong, 1997.
42. Aaker, 1996.
43. Leuthesser, Kohli and Suri, 2003.
44. Besharat and Langan, 2013.
45. Kotler and Armstrong, 2010.
46. Wernerfelt, 1988.
47. Anholt, 2005.
48. Leclerc, Schmitt and Dubé, 1994.
49. Han and Terpstra, 1988.

CHAPTER 2

BRANDING PRODUCTS

INTRODUCTION

Marketing today is a vastly different practice than it was even ten years prior. In fact, marketing has changed more in the past two years than in the past fifty years.[1] Information-rich marketers and constantly connected shoppers are changing the rules of long-held branding practices, yet one thing remains: Customers continue to attach meaning to brands that impacts on behavioral buying power according to Kevin Lane Keller. In an issue of the AMA Journal Reader, Keller summarizes a collection of branding related studies in the *Journal of Marketing* and analyzes how they identify with six key branding topics: brand elements, brand positioning, brand relationships, brand metrics, brand extensions, and brand management over time.[2] According to Keller, successful brands are backed up by successful products, and companies will engage in activities necessary to maintain that success through positive interactions that consumers have with a company and their products. He also makes the point that branding is both an art and a science, and marketers need to use any technological tool at their disposal to get a better understanding of the customer's behavior.[3]

The Kraft Heinz Corporation faced a crisis when two of its most successful brands, Jell-O and Oscar Mayer hot dogs, were threatened with the changing tastes of American consumers. As part of the merger between Kraft and Heinz has come the difficult task of determining where to put their resources, which brands to support, as well as which companies to acquire that house very successful brands. According to

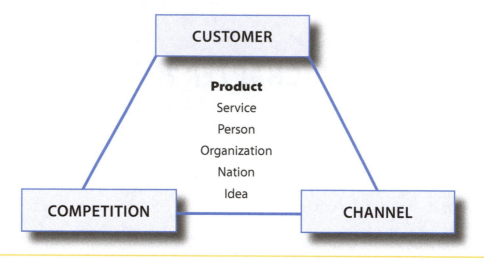

FIGURE 2.1 Strategic Brand Focus

the CEO Bernardo Hees, a corporation has to do whatever is necessary to continue to offer consumers great brands. As part of this strategy, Mr. Hees has been engaged in both re-shaping existing brands, as well as making offers to other corporations, like their unsolicited $143 billion offer for Unilever PLC, that sells brands including Axe deodorant, Dove soap, and Ben & Jerry's ice cream. In response to the offer from Kraft Heinz, there was a backlash against the offer from Unilever, who did not believe a merger made sense when the two organizations operate under such different business models. The point here is that at the heart of the decision-making of Kraft Heinz is the pursuit of great brands, and the steps necessary to maintain the market shares of brands that are underperforming because of changing consumer tastes.[4]

This chapter will address the branding of products, putting forward the first of the six brand entities highlighted in Figure 2.1. Whereas most people think of branding as it pertains to products, the analysis and case examples put forward in this chapter will lay the groundwork for the application of branding strategies to the other brand categories discussed in Chapters 3 to 7. There has, in fact, been a call for the boundaries of marketing to go beyond the traditional uses of it for products and services to other more non-traditional areas like politics, sustainability, and other areas that must also rely on some of the same tactics in an effort to wage successful strategic campaigns to bring about a desired change in their respective marketplaces.[5]

BUILDING STRONG BRAND LOYALTY

The goal of any organization that is selling a product is to create a unique brand identity that separates it from the competition. The process of separating your product in a way that makes it stand out in a positive light in the customer's mind usually ties into a few key product characteristics. In their classic book, *The 22 Immutable Laws of Branding: How to Build a Product or Service into a World-Class Brand,* the authors provide instructions on how to build a strong brand. According to their research, the consumer desires brands that are focused, authentic, and meaningful, and at the same time are perceived to be high quality.[6] With a successful branding strategy, a company is better positioned to effectively reduce the consumer's sensitivity to price by delivering value through quality, authenticity, and meaningfulness.

Ultimately, customer loyalty is what all companies seek to attain in their marketplace. Lin believes that customer loyalty is essential for long-term competitiveness and profitability of a product.[7] Jacoby and Olson were one of the earliest scholars to work on the subject of brand loyalty.[8] However, Lin reported that "affectional loyalty" has become a key evaluating factor of brand loyalty in modern branding. Behind his thinking lies the importance of building up trust with your customers, which has a more lasting impact if the customer has strong emotional ties to the product, service, or company in question. For example, it is clear that the Subaru automobile corporation has been very effective at building up a loyal following of customers whose strong emotional bond to the company helps to build up and support a following of like-minded, environmentally concerned individuals. At the same time, positive brand attitudes can also produce lasting brand loyalty.[9]

BRAND EXTENSIONS

Arslan and Altuna focused on brand extension into new categories of products.[10] According to their research, a recognized brand name with strong positive brand association creates and maintains a competitive advantage even in a highly competitive marketplace. Due to financial and other constrains associated with new product introduction, companies often introduce brand extensions instead of new brands. However, brand extensions can be risky and should therefore be created with caution. Unsuccessful brand extensions can be detrimental for the parent brand due to brand dilution, cannibalization, or brand failure. According to Martinez and de Chernatony, brand dilution is inevitable with brand extensions to an extent.[11] Brand dilution occurs when consumers' perceptions of the parent company or original product are changed. In other words, the brand of the product extension affects the brand of the original entity. The extent to which brand dilution detracts from overall brand equity defines its performance in the market.

When a brand is significantly diluted, its value falls. However, changing perceptions of a brand don't necessarily result in reduced brand equity overall, as perceived quality, familiarity with the brand, a good fit, and a positive attitude to the extension protect parent brand from negative effects of dilution. For example, when Ford manufactured their infamous Edsel, a car named after one of the sons of Henry Ford, it failed miserably. The failure had to do with the high level of expectations that were built up with Ford customers before the launch, who were let down after seeing the Edsel and not seeing it as a significant innovation. In effect, the perceived success of the car suffered because of the insufficient excitement that did not materialize after the launch of the car. After the original Edsel came out, it was followed by other similarly produced automobiles, with the same first name, Edsel, but a different second name.

Unfortunately for Ford, they lost a huge amount of money with the successive line of Edsels that followed because of the failure of the original model. Some models that followed were the Edsel Corsair, Edsel Pacer, Edsel Ranger, and Edsel Villager, all of which were ultimately doomed to fail because of the damaged brand image of Ford at that point in time. It was a well-known fact that Ford lost many millions of dollars due to the Edsel failure, and that alone helped to put a serious dent into sales. In Ford's case, the introduction of a perceived lower value model detracted from the strong Ford brand image, and hence customers associated Ford as a whole with the Edsel line.

On the other hand, cannibalization is another risk brands must thoughtfully consider in brand extension strategies. Cannibalization occurs when the new brand or product is not adequately differentiated from the original product and leads consumers to essentially replace the old brand with the new brand. It reduces sales and favorable perceptions of the old product in favor of the brand extension. Companies must therefore carefully consider the positioning of the product extension and ensure it is different enough as to avoid cannibalizing its own sales. The brand extension should offer a different enough type of value to be successful to a subset of customers, but not to drive away its existing customers. Companies must carefully weigh the perceived outcomes of a brand extension, and determine if it is in the entire company's best interest in the long run to risk introducing a product or service that would compete with itself.

By making an informed choice based on predicted consumer behaviors, brands can decide if cannibalization is a risk, or a potential benefit, to the company as a whole. Although a risk with potential to have severely damaging effects on a parent company or brand, there are also instances where cannibalization is a necessary part of growth.

For example, cannibalization is particularly common in the IT industry, and innovations in new cloud-based technologies serve as a relevant example. In the past five years, cloud computing has become an integral part of many business processes, and continuous advances in cloud computing technology have driven original cloud solution products obsolete in a very short amount of time. Salesforce, a Software-as-a-Service cloud provider and now industry leader specializing in customer relationship management (CRM) solutions, began as a CRM software targeting primarily small companies. Their initial products coincided well with small business needs, and were less complex and varied than their suite of products offered today. However, changing customer attitudes regarding security concerns about the cloud and a desire for more efficient business processes, coupled with sheer technological innovation and enhanced scalability led Salesforce to develop a wide array of products catered to large companies and is widely used among global corporations today. In essence, Salesforce's innovation eliminated its opportunity to compete for small business contracts, as the solutions it developed were too robust for a small business's needs. On the other hand, cannibalization of its initial products fueled the growth of the company, and Salesforce would not be as successful as it is today had they not decided to move forward with a product extension strategy.

BRAND PERSONALITY

According to Keller "brand resonance" is a relational component of branding that creates customer loyalty and strong brand affinity, which is crucial for success of the brand.[12] Relationships with brands and brand personalities are an important element of consumer branding. Research indicates that the relationships consumers form with brands are strengthened through brand personalities. Therefore, development of a brand personality should be at the forefront of developing an effective brand strategy for any given entity. In fact, according to Keller's research, consumers attribute "anthropomorphic" characteristics to brands, and relate to them as to personal beings.[13]

It is important to note that brand personality and brand identity are not identical terms, although they often are used interchangeably by scholars and practitioners. Azoulay and Kapferer defined brand personality as "the unique set of human personality traits both applicable and relevant to brands" and maintain that brand personality is part of brand identity.[14] They argue that qualities like competence, gender, and social class are not reliable components of brand personality, as they are not included by psychologists in human personality scales. Therefore, it is important to distinguish between the two terms.

BENEFITS AND RISKS OF EMOTIONAL BRANDING

An extension of brand personality ties into emotional branding, an area of research that is frequently used to create a strong brand loyalty for consumer goods. Emotional branding has proven to be a very effective branding tool by connecting products with the deepest needs of the customer to develop engaging and meaningful brand stories.[15]

In light of the fact that the consumer–brand relationship is an emotional bond built on trust, it is possible to elicit a strong negative response in the consumer if that trust is broken. Uber's tumultuous relationship with its consumers exemplifies how negative associations can impact brand equity. A series of public scandals, including inadequate pay and treatment of employees, accusations of sexism in the workplace, and inappropriate surge pricing during emergency events has negatively affected consumer brand perceptions and alienated potential consumers as a result. In fact, Uber is banned in several countries in part resulting from the strong negative response the brand emotions associated with the brand. The public backlash Uber has experienced since its inception has fueled social media campaigns including #DeleteUber and led consumers to abandon the brand altogether. When brands erode consumers' trust, as Uber has after a series of highly publicized scandals, the magnitude of consequences can be detrimental to the success of a brand as a whole. This is known by scholars as a doppelgänger brand image.[16] As noted by Holt, the doppelgänger brand image can create negative associations in the customer and prevent him/her from trusting the brand.[17] As evidenced by Uber's struggle to develop a brand perceived as trustworthy and honest, negative news spread fast, and anti-brand activism attracts a lot of attention in the popular media.

Clearly, once a doppelgänger appears, it is important for brand managers to take measures to restore brand image. It is crucial to monitor customer sentiments in the popular culture to identify the appearance of the doppelgänger brand image. Additionally, to mitigate any potential risks of emotional branding, it is important for brand managers to understand why their customers start showing the anti-brand behavior, and based on the finding, adjust the brand story accordingly. Consistent monitoring and consideration of the risks associated with emotional branding ought to be outlined throughout the brand strategy development process.

NEW ERA OF BRANDING

Branding is engrained in our culture. According to Gobe, the modern economy is focused on the consumer, and with the power of the Internet, branding is an active dialog with the consumer.[18] Moreover, traditional "push" communication has been replaced by "push and pull," with the Internet playing the major role in brand–consumer communication. This new dimension of branding is especially evident in the political marketplace where a candidate's personality oftentimes dominates the news cycles, moving from social media to the traditional media. Companies need to be willing to become vulnerable, as the digital space does not allow for harsh and unjust attitudes toward the consumer. One mistake in the dialog with the consumer can significantly damage the brand by creating a negative "chain reaction" and deterring the customer from the brand. There are several examples of this with passengers on airplanes who have been mistreated, videotaping the negative interaction and then sending it over the Internet and having it go viral.

According to the 2012 Edelman GoodPurpose® Study, Havas Media "Meaningful Brands" Global Report 2013, 2013 Deloitte Core Beliefs & Culture survey, and 2013 Cone Communications/Echo Global CSR Study, "87% of global consumers believe that business needs to place at least equal weight on society's interests as on businesses' interests."[19] Moreover, according to the Social Impact longitudinal study of Cone Communications, "89 percent of Americans are likely to switch brands to one associated with a cause, given comparable price and quality, jumping nearly 35 percent since 1993."[20] This is one of the new driving forces in the business world, and branding strategies must take this into account. The push for brands to appear holistic and overall beneficial to society has become an integral part of developing a relationship with the consumer. For example, it is becoming increasingly common for large corporations to boast social servitude, often in the form of company-wide volunteer days or charity match donation programs. Although these specific programs don't necessarily align with the primary business purposes these companies serve, they are an integral part of the brand strategy by creating a sense of good that consumers can relate to and feel good about. As more marketing campaigns and brand communications highlight a brand's charitable work or social values, consumers can develop a new level of trust by positively associating these good deeds with the overall brand, emulating trust and favorable brand perceptions.

Another key aspect of evolving U.S. culture is the increased use of celebrity endorsement as a branding technique. The use of easily recognizable celebrities is essential, according to Seno and Lukas.[21] Additionally, the celebrity endorsement must appear credible, or display "product-celebrity congruence." There is clearly a movement in this direction, for better and for worse. For example, during the 2016 U.S. Presidential Election, Hillary Clinton featured celebrities, like Beyoncé, George Clooney, Lady Gaga, and several others who appeared on stage with her, singing, supporting her, all with the intention of her building her brand from the sheer association with these high-profile people. This generated significant social buzz and created grassroots social media campaigns and trending hashtags including #ShesWithUs and #NotoriousHRC shared and discussed over social media by observers of these celebrity endorsements. Although her presidential campaign was unsuccessful, she built a reputation for her social media savviness and ability to connect with her supporters through the combination of celebrity figures amplified by social media channels.

DIGITAL MARKETING

In recent years, digital marketing efforts and e-commerce have experienced a rapid growth.[22] Online branding is different from traditional branding, where it is reported that as consumers acquire more experience by using the Internet, they will become more likely to search for alternative sources for information in such a user-friendly environment, and thus become less likely to revert to product branding as the sole basis for their choices in the marketplace.[23]

The benefits of e-commerce are the easy access of retailers to customers, along with a large variety of choices. However, e-commerce also has its drawbacks, such as the lack of differentiation that the abundance of retailers creates. Moreover, as consumers rely more and more on this retail medium, price wars become more prevalent. Finally, the intangibility of products that are sold online affect trust, and trust is one of the most important factors for online purchases.[24]

According to Melnik and Alm, with the intangibility of e-commerce and in the absence of reliable product information, buyers rely more on the reliability of the seller.[25] To survive in the online space, companies need to establish strong brands. Moreover, branding must be an active dialog with the consumer. In his 2001 published book, Gobe highlights "innovation, flexibility, and cultural relevance" as being defining elements of successful companies in the future. To effectively engage in a dialogue, companies should be willing to become vulnerable, as the digital space does not allow for harsh and unjust attitudes toward the consumer. One mistake in the dialog with the consumer can significantly damage the brand by creating a negative "chain reaction" and deterring the customer from the brand.[26]

According to Ward and Lee, consumers use brand names to infer the quality and value of a product sold online.[27] The big question for researchers and practitioners then becomes how to convey a sense of trust and product quality with information online. This could be one of the greatest challenges to product marketers who seek to compete in this retail space that do not come into it with a well-recognized company name and image.

QUANTIFYING BRAND VALUE

Effective branding has a direct effect on the company's financial performance. According to Aaker and Jacobson, stock returns grow as the brand quality improves.[28] Brand equity is a crucial component that lowers price elasticity and allows companies to be more flexible and effective in their advertising activities.[29]

According to Romero and Yagüe, "Brand equity and customer equity, respectively, constitute the value provided by brand and customer portfolios to companies."[30] Brand equity is directly connected with customer equity, as the right choices of products together with the loyalty of the right customers are two factors that drive growth, especially when resources are limited. Finding the "sweet spot" is crucial for both small companies and big corporations due to a strong competition and an abundance of similar offers.

If brands are so significant for the success of a modern business, it is crucial to measure the impact and manage it effectively. Multiple methods were created to measure the value of a brand. For example, marketers try to measure the cash flow that brands generate by comparing them to generic products with the same product characters.[31] Beckwith and Lehmann argue that the value of a brand depends not only on its objective characteristics, but also on the attitudes of consumers and popularity of the product, among many other subjective characteristics.[32] This phenomenon in marketing was derived from psychology and is called "halo effect."

Most would agree that the intangible value of a brand is hard to measure. Keller and Lehmann emphasized that the value of a brand is bigger than the value of its individual components.[33] It is important to emphasize that corporate branding has become a powerful tool to build brand equity of a company.[34] Corporations know that to attract the best talent and as well as an unconditional level of customer loyalty beyond price consideration, a company needs to develop a strong corporate brand. Today, customers want to support companies that make a positive impact in the society. Once that happens, the brand identity of those company's products become very attractive and lead to all of the positive outcomes identified in this chapter.

For example, the brand value of Nasty Gal, a web retailer founded by Sophia Amoruso, had a very rapid rise and fall in the online retail sector, as it became extremely popular with millennial shoppers. In the end, it succumbed to a bankruptcy filing after being in business for just under ten years, but not before the story can be told of an eBay vintage store that was turned into a company with $85 million in revenue in 2014. So, what happened, and how does this story pertain to its brand value? Working out of Los Angeles, it found itself with poor communication among employees, what many believed was the result of ineffective leadership at the top. But the most interesting part of this story is the value of the brand that was developed, even though the company went out of business. The company was able to sell its brand name as well as selected intellectual property for $20 million to a rival company working out of the U.K., Boohoo.com. The story of this startup and its fast rise to success is not the point here. So, even after going out of business due to internal difficulties, a company can still salvage the value of its brand name. The company eventually moved into a bricks-and-mortar outlet in Los Angeles in 2014, and opened up a store in Santa Monica in 2015. Some of the classic marketing problems faced by the company included a failure to adjust their product mix to an increasingly bigger customer base, as well as their decision to raise prices, difficult when trying to compete with fashion chains able to put out the latest styles at very competitive prices. It should also be pointed out that efforts to sell the store before bankruptcy filing was due to bad relationships with vendors, creating a problem for them as they tried to work with channel members.[35]

CASE STUDIES OF PRODUCT BRANDING

Case 1: TOMS Shoes

TOMS Shoes is a good example of a company that has succeeded on the basis of their branding strategy. By relying on the use of a purpose-driven marketing model, TOMS Shoes uses a "One for One" model. According to Geoffrey Precourt, "The most powerful brands are turning their initiatives to purpose-driven marketing."[36] Since its launch in 2006, TOMS Shoes has built a strong sustainable business model, based on the "One for One" community-based program (buy a pair of shoes from TOMS and a child in need gets a pair of shoes for free; buy a pair of TOMS eyewear, and TOMS will help to restore sight of a person in need). TOMS Shoes has centered its purpose-driven marketing model around the life-long relationship with its customer and the community. Building on this idea, "One for One" also provides a kind of value that most brands never can realize: internal satisfaction. The company has achieved great success, including:

- ▶ TOMS has given more than 10 million pairs of new shoes to children in need.
- ▶ TOMS has helped restore sight to more than 200,000 individuals around the world.

Zita Cassizzi, CEO of TOMS Shoes, created five action points for brands in search of a purposeful connection with the customer:

- ▶ Connect with your community
- ▶ Deliver content, products, and services
- ▶ Build customer relationships for life
- ▶ Continue the conversation for life
- ▶ Create a culture of innovation

According to Cassizzi, people are attracted to both giving and getting, and they expect companies to satisfy their need of a meaningful impact on the community. TOMS Shoes uses its resources to appeal to the customer in the digital space instead of spending a lot on traditional advertising. The company effectively targets millennials who spread the word with word of mouth (WOM). So prevalent is the social/mobile connection that Cassizzi's team has coined a phrase to describe it "Mocial." The company offers its customer an opportunity to "change the world," which meets the deepest human needs to relate and create a meaning.

Case 2: Procter & Gamble

For a company with a wide array of products and services, each individual product or service should appeal to a specific set of customers within the overall brand's target customer base. For example, P&G, a large consumer packaged goods company comprised of over seventy individual brands ranging from Olay to Pampers to Tide, cannot possibly appeal to just one type of customer with all of these different products. However, given the lack of a clear P&G branding strategy as a result of the company's focus on differentiating each of its brands in its portfolio individually, the company realized it was at risk of diluting the powerful P&G brand identity. The company therefore decided to focus on creating a cohesive branding strategy to support the P&G brand in addition to its various brand portfolios. Hence, the campaign run during the 2010 Olympics, "Proud Sponsor of Moms," gained traction. It was the company's biggest corporate campaign ever and the first to run on a global basis, and this message was splashed across digital marketing and social media channels, TV and radio ads, as well as print and billboard ads.[37]

Rather than attempt to resonate with various mom demographics across each of these brands, the simple message "Proud Sponsor of Moms" effectively integrated all brands relevant to their target with a unified, simple, and targeted slogan. What P&G effectively did was to recognize that their entire brand portfolio shared a common, general audience. However, this also provided extensive opportunity to further segment this target market by specific needs. P&G has declared its target audience as moms, but the mom shopping for Tide and the mom shopping for Olay are also different types of consumers with different needs. P&G's strategic push to generate cohesion while preserving differentiation in brand identities exemplifies the importance of understanding target market needs and effectively segmenting consumer groups further as needed for companies comprised of multiple brands.[38]

This strategy reflects on a key shift in branding that represents a move from branding individual products to branding a company as a whole. Given the unprecedented levels in which consumers can access information about a company's products, brands must deliver an aligned message for the entire entity, not just the specific piece of what is being sold. Although P&G is a parent company to literally thousands of disparate, unique consumers' packaged goods, all of its products are rolled up into the unified message that the company strives to support moms. This message cascades down into its products, as diapers, dish soap, beauty goods, etc., are all products its target would use, so it effectively accomplishes the task of advertising its individual products while maintaining a favorable perception of all of the brands in P&G's portfolio. Therefore, a mom could feel just as supported by purchasing a box of Pampers as she could by purchasing a bottle of Dawn dish soap.

Although these products have two entirely different uses, the consumer associates them with the same positive, supportive message from P&G as a whole. Of course, this is just one example, though the shift to messaging the parent company applies across multiple industries. In the B2B sector, ExxonMobil, Dow, Google, and IBM, to name a few, have successfully utilized the corporate brand story to strengthen their brands.

STRATEGIC BRAND FOCUS

By knowing what your customer desires as well as understanding their behaviors, brands can identify what messaging is most appropriate and how to reach them. For large brands offering diversified products/services/brand attributes, effective segmentation is a critical component of understanding the customer. Market segmentation effectively allows brands to target specific pieces of the brand or product to specific subsets of customers.

In an effort to successfully analyze the current competitive state of affairs, brands must be keenly aware of the tactics employed by competitors and monitor how well they are resonating with the audience. In addition to keeping a watchful eye on the competition, companies must also understand how to help the customer understand how their product differs from a competitor's product. Identifying and communicating key differences creates a competitive advantage, which drives adoption, support, and purchase of a given product, service, idea, etc. In tandem with competitive analysis should be a customer and channel strategy consideration, as these three aspects together when all three are clearly defined and aligned, drive brand excellence and success. The importance of thoroughly analyzing your target consumer base to understand their behaviors is critical in channel selection. Your brand needs to not only be present where your target consumers are, but it also needs to be present in a way that resonates with your target consumer.

For example, if one were to compare the tactics used in previous U.S. presidential elections to the ones used in the most recent campaigns, it would become obvious that there have been major changes in the choice of channels of communications used by political organizations. Going back to 1960, when politics was revolutionized by the use of television, many attributed Kennedy's success and appeal as a candidate that was conveyed through the first debates held on television. As Nixon and Kennedy debated, perspiration was developing on Nixon's upper lip, which was obvious to the person watching it. In fact, in research carried out after the debate, those who listened to it on the radio thought Nixon had won, but those who watched it on television thought Kennedy won.

The point is that the channel of communication played a key role in defining each of these respective candidates' brands in the minds of American voters. The American public was largely attuned to television at this point in history, and thus Kennedy's successful execution of his television persona, which carried with it a strong visual representation of confidence, eloquence, and intelligence displayed through the televised debates, made him appear presidential in the public's eyes. At this point in time, television as a marketing channel had enormous influence on consumers because most Americans had television sets in their homes, and watched it frequently. However, as technology has continued to play an increasingly more important role in the communication of all products, the American public today has largely shifted its attitudes and behaviors toward television commercials. They no longer resonate as well, and the number of TV sets in American households has been steadily declining, and with that change, has come the popularity of the use of the Internet which has created new platforms for information exchange, communication, and advertising methods. As a result, we've seen the increasing importance of social media as an effective channel used by organizations to reach their targeted consumers with their products.

CONCLUSION

In developing any effective branding strategy, it is imperative to have a clear brand focus, which encompasses brand characteristics, messaging, and channels, and ensures each of these elements are aligned and support each other. Strategic identification of effective marketing channels largely impacts consumer perceptions of a given brand. In other words, the brand must be where its target audience is, which requires thorough analysis of target consumer group behaviors, communication preferences, and attitudes regarding various marketing channels.

Emotional branding is a powerful tool for organizations to market their brands to selected customers and, over time, this helps a company to establish and reinforce relationships over the long term. Although emotional branding certainly has the influence to drive positive relationships, if executed improperly, emotional branding can also be detrimental to the development of brand–consumer relationships. When brands exemplify behaviors or values that are not aligned with how the consumers view them, the dissonance between the brand's actions and the consumer's previously positive view of the brand creates a deep sense of mistrust and essentially reverses brand loyalty. Companies that take the time to carry out consumer and marketing research studies will be best positioned to leverage this important factor in the branding of products. With the multiple meanings that can accrue to a given product, making the correct connections with emotions that have resonance with a specific market segment will insure the likelihood of continued use of the product, and a brand loyal following that is at the heart of all marketing strategies.

To a great degree, the art and science of branding is very much focused on those products that allow companies to develop creative platforms from which to operate on. One example of this kind of creative thinking was the partnership between Kraft Heinz and Oprah Winfrey, whose product line definitely expanded the reach and reputation of Kraft Heinz, who will continue to be known for the new brands they bring into the market. Along with the nutritious food items that Oprah Winfrey brings to the table will be the unique recipes she has a reputation for developing. This example represents what all corporations must constantly be engaged in, which is the development and maintenance of brands that represent the latest consumer tastes, as well as decisions on mergers and acquisitions of other companies that insures their competitive position in a market. Every corporation needs a plan for profitable growth, and whichever steps are necessary to do that often centers on the choice of which brands to support, and which companies to acquire. Brands not only represent growth for a corporation in an existing market, but in the global marketplace that exists today, the choice of brands to support often centers on the opportunity it creates for a corporation to take it worldwide.[39]

Endnotes

1. Adobe, Marketing has changed more in the past two years than in the past 50 n.d.
2. K. L. Keller, 2003.
3. Udell, 2014.
4. Gasparro, 2017.
5. Newman, 2002.

6. Ries and Ries, 2009.
7. Lin, 2010.
8. Jacoby and Olson, An attitude model of brand loyalty: Conceptual underpinnings and instrumentation research, 1970.
9. Louis and Lombart, 2010.
10. Arslan and Altuna, 2010.
11. Martinez and de Chernatony, 2004.
12. K. L. Keller, 2003.
13. Keller and Lehmann, 2006.
14. Azoulay and Kapferer, 2003.
15. Thompson, Rindfleisch and Arsel, 2006.
16. Thompson, et al., 2006.
17. Holt, Why do brands cause trouble? A dialectical theory of consumer culture and branding, 2002.
18. Gobe, 2001.
19. Mainwaring, 2013.
20. Cone Communications n.d.
21. Seno and Lukas, 2007.
22. Ward and Lee, 2000.
23. Ward and Lee, 2000.
24. Ward and Lee, 2000.
25. Melnik and Alm, 2002.
26. Gobe, 2001.
27. Ward and Lee, 2000.
28. Aaker and Jacobson, 1994.
29. Keller and Lehmann, 2006.
30. Romero and Yagüe, 2015.
31. Shocker and Weitz, 1988; Fischer n.d.; Shankar, Azar and Fuller, 2008.
32. Beckwith and Lehmann, 1975.
33. Keller and Lehmann, 2006.
34. Rao, Agarwal and Dahlhoff, 2004.
35. Chaney, 2017.
36. Precourt, 2014.
37. Marshall and Wise, 2013.
38 Marshall and Wise, 2013.
39 Gasparro, 2017.

CHAPTER 3

BRANDING SERVICES

INTRODUCTION

Services are different from goods with respect to the fact that they are intangible, heterogeneous, inseparable, and perishable, according to Fisk, Brown, and Bitner.[1] Unlike a product, services cannot be held and inspected, as they are intangible by definition. Services also vary by nature because they are normally delivered by a person. However, in light of the fact that these conclusions by respected scholars in the field of marketing go back several decades, it is important to fast-forward to the current point in time when some services are now being delivered vis-à-vis the Internet with advances in IT. For example, online banking, phone application management, reservation/project management software, etc., are all services that are shifting to less person-based and more technology-based. But the fact still remains that there are an abundant number of services still delivered by humans, and in light of this, one must still take into account this significant difference that exists between the delivery of products and services.

Furthermore, a service is often inseparable from the service provider, whether it is a haircut being given by a stylist, or a checkup provided by a doctor. Finally, a service is perishable, as it cannot be stored in the same way that a can of soup can on a supermarket shelf. These unique characteristics make branding a service more complicated than the branding of products, as it becomes more difficult to promote brands that do not have a physical entity to put into advertisements and commercials.

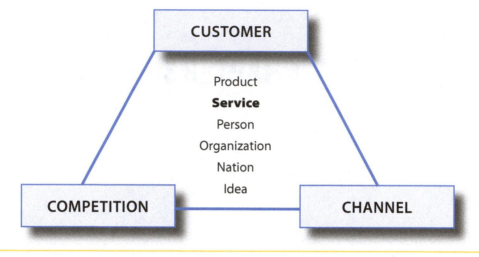

FIGURE 3.1   **Strategic Brand Focus**

However, some scholars have argued that goods can be considered "service appliances" as customers experience their "service" in use.[2] This argument puts forward the thesis that the interaction between the company and the customer is a continual process of creating and recreating brand value.[3] If an organization were to follow this line of thinking, managers can use this approach to treat customers as co-creators of their offerings by using both a pre-sale and post-sale pitch.

Davis believes that the service sector has not received enough attention from scholars.[4] As the author notes, clients of service companies do not always consciously associate the company name with its brand. He makes the further point that the quality of services cannot be assessed before they are consumed, and since brand equity is an indicator of quality used by customers, risk-averse customers are likely to choose well-known service providers. These findings also support the classic works of Berry and Berry, Lefkowith, and Clark.[5, 6] From a marketing standpoint, one could then argue that brand equity plays an even more crucial role in service branding, and thus creating a strongly favored consumer brand in the services sector determines the success of the brand in the marketplace.

What further complicates the branding of a service is the fact that even within a single service-oriented organization, the quality may significantly differ due to different providers offering the service, which one could find in a chain of restaurants across the country. But even with this possibility, strong brand equity can help reduce the risks of negative customer experiences. For example, this becomes a very important issue in the hotel industry, where a person may have a negative experience that is not attributed to the overall hotel brand, but rather to a certain location or service provider where the negative experience took place.[7] If one makes the argument that branding is a relationship between the company and the customer, then service branding is a relationship where the need for trust is even bigger due to the intangibility of services and an increased risk of a purchase, among other factors.

SUCCESSFUL SERVICE BRANDING

According to many scholars and marketing practitioners, customer satisfaction is in the center of a successful service brand.[8, 9] Booms and Bitner point out that the traditional 4Ps marketing mix (product, price, promotion, and place) should be expanded with three more elements for service brands: customer service, people, and process.[10,11] Marketers know that services provide more intimate interactions with the customers, and customers do care about choosing the right service provider.

Brand equity is a very effective way for customers to infer the level of quality in a service.[12] In an effort to reduce the level of risk, customers are likely to choose well-known service providers because they convey certain expected positive attributes. Ballantyne and Aitken make the point that whereas a brand conveys promises, customers and other stakeholders explicitly re-create the brand as a "social construct."[13] In light of this, companies oftentimes try to instill a certain brand image in the minds of customers. However, the initiatives may become unsuccessful if the company is not focused on the customer. Since the meaning of a brand is created in the minds of consumers, the only true brand image is the one that a company's customers develop, not the one that corporations seek to develop. So ultimately, the real risk for any service organization is to assume that their brand is defined in their customer's mind in the same way that they sought to create the meaning of it.

The fact of the matter is that service companies do have the ability to customize their offerings to meet the unique needs and wants of a client better than a product brander can, because of the intimate relationship that can build over time between provider and customer. The additional attention paid to the customer in a service-related encounter helps to create a more positive response and to bring about a greater desire on the part of the customer to continue doing business with a service provider. Moreover, many services differentiate their brands based on their customer service initiatives.

For example, in the travel industry, there are a variety of levels of customer service various companies offer that differentiate one type of vacation from another.

In the cruise line industry, there are many companies that cater to different vacation experiences. Carnival cruise ships are known for their lower priced fares, large ships to accommodate hundreds of travelers, and celebratory feel. In contrast, Seabourn cruise ships are much smaller, accommodating far fewer passengers, provide a customized, specialized feel for customers, and have a more relaxed environment. Seabourn cruises, given their high levels of personalization and customer service, are priced quite a bit higher than Carnival cruises. Seabourn seeks to deliver a very personalized level of service and focuses on building relationships with customers onboard, whereas Carnival's cruise ships are not conducive to providing such highly individualized and personal experiences. Since the strategic focus of service branding is often centered around the relationship that ensues with a customer, organizations strive to create a positive experience every time a customer interacts with the service brand.[14] For example, Seabourn employees are required to memorize the names of the guests on each floor of the ship and greet them by name each time they see them. This level of intimacy aims to establish a connection between guests onboard and employees, as well as reinforce a positive experience with the brand that equates Seabourn with extraordinary levels of customer service.

In one study carried out by de Chernatony and Riley, they interviewed twenty reputable brand consultants to examine how service branding differs from product branding, and what branding concepts are common for products and services.[15] As the authors discovered, there exists a substantial inconsistency in the branding of services, which implies that the agreement on the best strategy to use is not consistent across service sectors. The authors suggested that the inconsistency that exists in this branding area can be eliminated by adopting brand strategies built on a strong customer focus and excellent internal communication within a company. In another study carried out by de Chernatony and Segal-Horn, they examined interviews that were carried out with twenty-eight leading brand consultants who shared their expertise in service branding.[16] Based on the analysis, the authors identified that total services brand experience, social processes, and internal consistency are the key factors in effective branding of services.

It is obvious that each of the studies reported on what makes a service brand successful is the result of the rather complex environment that service operators exist in, and the need on the part of scholars in the field to isolate what they consider to be the leading contributors, or the best practices that exist in this sector that brings about success.

One could conclude from these studies that service branding is exposed to multiple factors that operate both within and outside these organizations, and to be successful, there must be an effort made to tie together the internal and external factors at play. It is also worth mentioning that the role of the management is crucial for the success of all service companies regardless of their size, as it is the management that has the responsibility of choosing the right brand and communication strategy and staffing to plan the budget, as well as to delegate responsibilities across employees in the organization. It is imperative for management to be an integral part of developing service branding strategy given the impact of their influence.

As several countries, including the United States, continue to shift from a manufacturing focus to a service dominated economy, the implications of successful service branding will continue to become more important for brands to understand and effectively navigate in order to survive in an increasingly competitive environment.

RISKS IN SERVICE BRANDING

Since positive experiences create loyal customers and spread a positive word about the service provider, negative experiences can ultimately be detrimental to a service business. Although this is not any different than for a product brander, there is some evidence that a dissatisfied service customer is more likely to share their displeasure with others than a product user might who is dissatisfied. According to the annual Brandz study by Millward Brown, in the service market, customer dissatisfaction often leads to negative reviews and recommendations.[17] As branding practitioners argue, unmet expectations are destructive for a service brand.[18] Since services are not standardized in the same way that products are, sold in the identical package with the exact same ingredients, it is more than likely that a customer seeking to use the service of an organization will use their past experiences as a barometer to measure their satisfaction of a current encounter, which could be variable based on the unique characteristics of a service. Given the innate variation in experiences services offer as opposed to the relatively standardized experience packaged goods offer, there is greater opportunity for experiences to differ among individuals, and potentially amplify the negative service encounters consumers have with a brand.

It is important to emphasize that the risks discussed above can and should be managed by means of best business practices. Since the delivery of a service provider can take place through different people each time a customer interacts with a company, it is in the best interests of the service organization to build up strong brand equity in an effort to reduce the potential negative effects of variability.[19] Therefore, effective and talented leaders can successfully manage the service variability using the right metrics and incentives, and nurturing a healthy corporate culture.[20] For example, a clever coach of a major sports team competing in any number of different sports venues, whether it is baseball, basketball, or football for example, is in a position to deflect the losing performance of the team during a portion of the season by being able to create a positive culture across the members of the team, and insuring that each person on the team does not begin to blame one another for losses.

In a similar vein, employees who work for an airline who operate in different capacities from greeting the flyer at the desk in the airport, to the stewardesses and stewards who work on the plane, can help to create a more positive experience for the flyer if they are all imparting the same positive attitude toward the flyers. This is especially important in a sector where it is likely that the customer will be impacted by unexpected levels of discomfort, like a flight delay or an unruly flyer sitting next to them. An airline we can draw an example from is the level of service Spirit Airlines provides its customers. Notorious for low levels of service in exchange for lower ticket prices, Spirit does not meet many of the basic service requirements most major airlines offer, such as a stewardess to greet passengers, complimentary beverages onboard the plane, and free ticket printing upon airport arrival. Although the benefit to the consumer for Spirit's services is lower airfares, the infamously poor levels of customer service are associated with the brand, earning it the nickname "Crush you Spirit" Airlines. It is unclear at this time as more lower-fare airlines enter the competitive market how poor levels of customer service will impact Spirit's brand. It is entirely possible they will be forced to shift their strategy to be more accommodating as a result.

Loyalty in the service market is a complex relational phenomenon. According to Hollis, customer satisfaction does not necessarily equate with customer loyalty.[21] Loyal customers are willing to "forgive" a service brand if something goes wrong, as a person is willing to forgive his/her good friend who made a mistake, because there exists a trust and a shared value that is not easy to replace or replicate. This is frequently observed in politics. When consumers are loyal to politicians they favor, they are more willing to forgive errors or policies that do not align with their personal values. For example, during Donald Trump's presidential campaign, tape recordings were leaked of him making highly inappropriate and lewd comments about women. His own campaign could not deny these statements were made, so they were forced to address them as an isolated incident on Trump's part. His campaign manager, Kellyanne Conway, addressed this issue publicly from a woman's perspective and clearly stated that although she does not condone the statements he made, argued that it was a single observance and does not represent Trump's general demeanor toward women. It appears as though many of his female supporters were willing to forgive him as well, given that his election garnered nearly 50 percent of the vote from Caucasian women specifically. Given the enormous impact this could have had on his brand, the loyalty his supporters felt toward his campaign ultimately drove them to continue to support him as a candidate, and loyalty to the Trump brand ultimately resulted in an electoral victory in November 2016.

BRAND PERSONALITY IN SERVICE BRANDING

One of the more prolific authors in this area has been the work of Berry, who made the argument that service branding should be focused on trust-building and positive reputation.[22] Berry recommends that service companies create a distinct brand and emotional connection with their customers. With respect to external brand communications, word of mouth and publicity play a key role in the successful branding of a service. He also highlights the importance of cultivating a strong company culture to sustain the healthy service brand from within.

Grace and O'Cass argue that brand names significantly reduce the perceived risk associated with some service sectors.[23] For example, one of the perceived strengths of McDonald's is the consistency that one can assume will exist regardless of which McDonald's restaurant one goes to. But the question remains, which is: How can a company create strong service brands? According to their Service-Branding Verdict Model (SBV), it is possible to build strong service brands if the correct branding strategy is followed. Their model represents a holistic view of service branding, relying on the following brand dimensions: Brand name; core product/service; feeling and experiences; price; user imagery; and communications and advertising. The model has in fact integrated the previous research findings of Keller and Berry.[24, 25] Each of the brand dimensions can be used to create a more consistent brand experience with a service operator that helps that organization to overcome the variability and intangibility that is characteristic of this brand category.

SERVICE BRAND WEBSITES

Websites devoted to a brand (aka, brand sites) are a popular tool to promote service brands and develop strong customer relationships and loyalty.[26] As many scholars argue, intangibility and a "high level of perceived risk" are two characteristics of service brands that makes them different from product brands.[27, 28] Because of this, service brand websites need to create a certain level of tangibility to eliminate the psychological risks involved, and to build customer trust.

An increasingly important way to build trust is through user experience focused web design to create user-friendly and easily navigable websites. As previously discussed, the digital landscape is constantly shifting, and therefore brand sites must stay relevant with these changes. To illustrate the importance of user experience from a design standpoint, consider the impact of responsive websites. As search engine traffic from mobile devices has exceeded desktop searches over the past several years, with projections of continued exponential growth, the increase to mobile friendly design has become increasingly imperative. Today, consumers expect to be able to access user optimized websites from their mobile devices. If websites are not mobile optimized, they are ranked lower in organic search engine result rankings and have astronomical bounce rates when accessed from mobile devices, meaning once users click on a site from a mobile device and see it is non-responsive, they immediately leave the site. Users must be able to interact with and navigate the site easily and intuitively, thus mobile-first design is a key trend to consider given digital consumer behavior trends. Additional design elements tend to change based on trends. For example, pop-up interstitials (full page ads that appear before the destined webpage) were very commonplace in websites three years ago. Today, websites aim to create a streamlined experience, and the use of pop-ups interrupts user experiences, hence this trend is no longer a best website practice. Given that customer demands are always changing, aligning web presences to meet these needs is an imperative first step in creating an effective digital branding presence.

Dou and Krishnamurthy looked at the concept of brand sites in service industries.[29] They believe that service brand sites should be built to reduce the customer's "psychological barriers associated with intangibility and perceived risk of service brand." In addition to creating a user-friendly brand site, brands must also include strong content. Today's consumer has access to more information through the Internet than ever before, meaning they have the ability to research, shop around, and compare against competitors. Therefore, differentiation must be a key component of content strategy. Consumers must be able to easily identify the unique value a brand can bring them through the website. Davis, Buchanan-Oliver, and Brodie highlight the importance of convenience and information-oriented experiences to drive online experiences.[30]

Furthermore, the virtual reality technologies and their future (e.g., the recent purchase of Oculus VR by Facebook) can transform both the product and service industry by changing how consumers reach and interact with brands. Mark Zuckerberg, the CEO of Facebook, in his statement on Oculus VR: "After games, we're going to make Oculus a platform for many other experiences. Imagine enjoying a courtside seat at a game, studying in a classroom of students and teachers all over the world or consulting with a doctor face-to-face—just by putting on goggles in your home."[31]

SERVICE EXPERIENCE AND TRUST

Modern service branding is rapidly transforming other industries. The importance of reputation, trust, and genuine care that has long been recognized in the service marketing, is now being adopted by traditionally non-service oriented companies. The principle of trust still remains crucial in service branding because services are more intimate in nature, and therefore elements like trust and authenticity are particularly important to consumers. Nigel Hollis, chief global analyst at the market research firm Millward Brown, for example, argued that to create a strong service brand, the customer must believe there is a fair exchange happening, and that the service justifies the cost of it. Strong brand loyalty is grounded in repeated positive interactions with brands. In other words, the framework can be described as: Purchase—Feel Good—Repeat. Consider the role of a hairstylist as it pertains to this framework. When one goes to a new hairstylist for the first time, they expect to be able to leave with the style, cut, or color they envisioned. If the stylist is able to deliver the service that meets client expectations, clients leave satisfied with their service. The next time they make an appointment, they are likely to return to the same stylist given the level of satisfaction they have come to expect based on previous positive experiences. Thus, the cycle repeats itself and continues, creating a loyal customer driven by the level of trust he or she established with the stylist.

RELATIONSHIP MARKETING

Whereas the field of relationship marketing is by no means a new discovery, it does play a very important role in better understanding how to succeed as a service brander. Dall'Olmo and de Chernatony reported that the increasingly important role that relationship marketing plays in all customer exchanges at a service level, in addition to the rapid movement in e-commerce for all organizations has prompted companies of different sizes "to seek direct relationships with the consumers."[32] The authors empha-size that corporate brand identity is crucial for modern service businesses, and argue that ultimately the service brand building process is a combination of the relationship that exists between the organization and its employees, as well as the relationship taking place between the consumer and the employees of the service provider.

The research shows that for a lasting relationship to exist, both the customer and the company must realize that there are benefits that will result from participating in the relationship. In order to cultivate and deepen relationships across various channels and mediums, brands must create effective consumer touch points. In other words, brands must be present and encouraging of consumer-brand interactions. We see this particularly in the digital space, with consumer-brand interactions across social media channels, blogs, and consumer review websites and applications like Yelp. However, event marketing, surveying, and call centers are also methods brands use to create additional touch points.

As we see the increase in brand–consumer interactions, both parties derive benefit by establishing and deepening these relationships. Consumers want their voices to be heard and find ease of communication with brands through these touch points. On the other hand, brands have the ability to gain valuable insights from the increased communication, creating a mutually beneficial relationship. Consider the importance of relationship marketing as it pertains to politics. Politicians running for office encourage consumer participation in shaping their policy decisions and key issues upon which they will base their campaign and messaging. Politicians understand that in order to get elected, they must create value for the general public who holds the voting power. Establishing a brand rooted in shared values strengthens community relationships, enhances a candidate's social and political capital, and ultimately increases their chances of winning an election. From a consumer standpoint, the public's vote is determined by how well a candidate aligns with their personal values and political views. Therefore, consumers find value having a voice in these decisions, which is why successful politicians who are focused on forming relationships with voters and their communities throughout the campaign process tend to be the candidate that gets elected.

POLITICAL MARKETING

One of the more recent developments in the service marketing discipline is the application of marketing to politics. In this chapter, we introduce this topic as a prime example of how services, or the intangible offering of a set of benefits from an organization to a group of customers, relies heavily on branding as a mechanism to differentiate the unique image of one politician from another, or from one political party to another. Political marketing can be defined as "the application of marketing principles and procedures in political campaigns by number of individuals and organizations." The procedures involved include the analysis, development, execution, and management of strategic campaigns by candidates, political parties, governments, lobbyists and interest groups that seek to drive public opinion, advance their own ideologies, win elections, and pass legislation and referenda in response to the needs and wants of selected people and groups in a society.[33]

The political landscape has shifted drastically over the past several decades, but arguably the more so in the past three election cycles than any other point in history. Why is this? Candidates are placing more of an emphasis than ever on marketing themselves to the general public. In the digital age, personal branding has become more important than ever before. The 24/7 news cycle, made effective in large part through the Internet, requires candidates to continuously market themselves in all activities they do, from philanthropy to rallies to fundraising events, the public can see all of it. This is in part why the advertising budgets have doubled each election cycle in the past four cycles. Voters are demanding and consuming the marketing efforts laid out by political candidates, and establishing and reinforcing a political brand that resonates with the largely diverse voter base which has become a key component of any political marketing strategy.

Candidates also have more channels in which to access the general public. Relatively newly developed marketing channels replace what was historically effective in past elections. Gone are the days of telemarketers and direct mail campaigns. These marketing techniques are being replaced with social media campaigns, grassroots efforts, Internet advertising, and text messaging campaigns. The way in which a candidate connects with and speaks to the public is shifting, creating a completely new political dynamic and redefining the election process altogether. The public has greater access to knowledge about political candidates than ever before. The Internet allows us to thoroughly research each candidate's background, political history, and personal scandals, which shapes our view and ultimately impacts our voting stances. Because voters are more informed than ever before, the importance of investing in creating and reinforcing political brands largely shape our political views.

Big data, a relatively new buzzword that captures the opportunity digital technologies can provide, was a cornerstone in both of Barack Obama's successful presidential campaigns, and more recently it was leveraged in both Donald Trump and Hillary Clinton's 2016 campaigns. Thanks to big data, candidates have the ability to collect and mine data on voters to decipher the issues they care about and how to reach them. They can also more effectively pinpoint where to most efficiently spend their advertising dollars, focusing most intently on securing undecided voters and continuing to build relationships with committed voters as well. With increased access to data and enhanced micro-targeting capabilities, candidates can more effectively tap into the interests of the nation and essentially advertise themselves to align with our values. As a result, we are more connected than ever with our political candidates, thanks to advances in data mining and application. With greater access to information, political scandals seem to occur more frequently than ever. Crisis management skills of candidates has become a critical and arguably high stakes skill that candidates are required to possess in order to stay in the race.[34]

If one were to compare the marketing of politicians to any other group of professionals, there are many similarities, including the fact that a politician, like a doctor or lawyer, seeks to create a brand identity in the market, in this, the political marketplace, where the politician is differentiated from his or her competition through personality and leadership characteristics, and policies that help to define that individual.[35] One of the key distinctions that exists in political marketing is the actual delivery of the service, which can take place when a politician is running for political office, as well as when a politician is running a government, sometimes referred to as the permanent campaign, where strategists from a campaign enter into public office with the winning elected official as an advisor. This distinction sets up one of the most important differences in branding in this discipline.

The branding strategy used during a political campaign is operating under a very different set of pressures and constraints than the branding strategy used once a candidate wins office, particularly when the office is the White House. A campaign is by definition an operation that exists under a microscope, where every utterance of the politician is scrutinized, reviewed, and shared on social media websites. One need not look any farther than the 2016 U.S. Presidential Elections when the country witnessed Donald Trump using Twitter to communicate with millions of followers, thereby circumventing the traditional media. This is a critical point from a branding perspective given the fact that the traditional media in the U.S. have played such an important role in defining the image, and ultimately, the brand of a candidate running for the presidency.

Once the candidate enters the White House, once again the rules change significantly by which a successful branding strategy must be used, taking into account the multitude of opinion leaders and outside entities who could impact on the brand identity of a president, from other foreign leaders, to the opposition leaders, to political action committees and interest groups who have an ax to grind with the policies of the president. All recent presidents in the U.S. have witnessed a barrage of criticism from the public soon after entering into office when policies are put into place that have a negative impact on their respective social group. This is a more complex branding situation that calls for all of the insights that were identified earlier in this chapter.

Politicians operate in a very dynamic market situation, and do not have the luxury of branding their individualistic form of ideology against just one other organization, but instead have to operate in an environment that is full of differing voices that can change in a matter of seconds if a crisis occurs. Just take the case of 9/11, when President George W. Bush was faced with the greatest threat to the U.S. since the attack that took place at Pearl Harbor. The president's brand also took a significant change during the years immediately following 9/11, which many would argue was in part for his successful re-election campaign because he was judged to have done a good job in office dealing with that crisis. So, a key difference in political marketing that separates it from other more traditional organizations operating in both the for-profit and non-profit arenas has to do with the number and severity of crises that have to be dealt with. In a sense, this unique characteristic that exists in political marketing puts even more importance on the role of branding in insulating the consistency of message and image during difficult periods. If one were to compare political marketing with other organizations, the conclusion is that it has more in common with service and nonprofit organizations than with corporations selling products.

As service providers, all politicians are making promises to citizens, whether it is during a campaign or after they enter the office they won. In a sense, this separates the role of the political marketer from other service providers because the promises that are used to win office are usually the barometer that is used to determine the success of the operation. This is unlike any other service provider whose brand is justified on the sheer basis of how much revenue is generated over a period of time, especially on a consistent basis from the same customers. In effect, as with all service providers, the performance of the politician is what determines success or failure, but the performance of a politician is judged on many more different levels than a more traditional service provider. But just as a company is always concerned with making promises to attract new customers, so must a politician who needs to win over a critical mass to get elected, and expand that base once in office to insure re-election.

CASE STUDIES OF SERVICE BRANDING

Case 1: Ritz-Carlton Hotel

There are many examples in the service sector of organizations that have excelled due to their branding strategies. The Ritz-Carlton Hotel represents an organization that has taken advantage of some of the more recent technological advances in the service sector that has enabled the company to flourish in multiple markets where the competitive environment is extremely challenging. This service-oriented organization represents a generation of firms that have been in existence for many years now, but have been able to stay competitive through a reliance on technology. The hotel industry is now subject to competitors like AirBnB, who have eroded the market share of the traditional hotels through the use of the Internet as a communication channel, and new distribution channels that rely on alternative places for tourists to stay, like private apartments and homes as an alternative to a hotel room that uses rates that undercut traditional hotels by as much as 50 percent or more.

In the world of hotels, one could make the case that a brand like The Ritz-Carlton represents a model of customer service in today's business world that exudes branding success through their stylistic use of customer service that has advanced over the years through the use of constant upgrading, and always keeping its brand in touch with what customers of all ages seek, whether it is a Baby Boomer seeking elegance in a hotel, or a very casual millennial looking for something slightly different than what they would seek in a more traditional hotel.[36]

Case 2: Uber

Uber has disrupted the taxi industry with their innovative use of mobile applications to make a direct contact with potential customers that is convenient and cost effective. However, when it comes to its branding strategy, there is much left to be desired. Part of their problem also lies with their inability to establish a uniform global brand identity as they move from one country to another with respect to the use of one logo that is standardized, with the same color and palette. However, it is not surprising to find this situation with such a new company. The company has moved so fast, now operating in over sixty countries, this is an institutional issue that must be addressed at the very top of the organization, and brings into play the very important role of re-branding, which Uber has been engaged in as it moves at supersonic speed across the world.

One could argue that Uber is in the midst of a transformation as they grow so quickly, thus throwing them into a certain state of confusion as they seek to create a brand identify for their services that will support the very fast growth of the company. On the one hand, Uber wants to be seen as more than just a taxi service (such as their movement into the restaurant delivery sector with Uber Eats, where they are delivering food to customers), and without a well explained narrative, in writing, by the CEO to get this point across to customers, it makes their job of finding a symbol to express this very difficult. In the end, a company has to know who they are, the kind of company they want to be, and where they are headed. Without that clarity, it becomes very difficult to express this in a brand logo.[37]

Case 3: LinkedIn

To the professional, there may be nothing more important than the ability to express who you are with a profile and network that reflects on that. Welcome to the world of LinkedIn, where individuals can use this technological application to advance their career, stay connected with their network, and use the services of this organization whenever they need to. In effect, this company provides professionals with a personal brand identity that no other company has yet developed. Through the use of this social media platform, clients can engage in a long-range effort to maintain their career profile over time. LinkedIn was the very first company to offer their users an online resume that has grown into a customized branding management tool. In effect, it is a catch-all for many roles that before this company was started was carried out by different sources. It serves as a personal agent, recruiter, and public relations firm for those that use the services it offers.[38]

STRATEGIC BRAND FOCUS

From the point of view of a strategic focus on the branding of services, there will be some unique characteristics that stand out as different from product branding. For example, the customer's needs and wants may be more difficult to satisfy if there is the possibility for the delivery of the service to vary from one time to another. Just take the case of a person going to get their hair styled by the same person month after month. There is always that risk that the stylist will not deliver the same quality of service each time a customer walks into the shop. This then creates a pressure on the part of the service provider, in this case the hairstylist, to enlist other factors that could be used to keep a customer satisfied with other benefits that come with going to the same stylist, such as have a friendly conversation with the client, or even offering new ideas on how the client can cut their hair if they are looking for a change.

It is this unpredictability due to the variation that occurs in a human-based service delivery that makes this C (Customer) a critical component from a strategic standpoint. By the customer knowing that there will be a consistency of delivery of a haircut/style that can be expected each time he/she goes to visit the stylist, the credibility of the stylist increases, and along with that, the positive emotional connection with the person who delivers the service. Ultimately, this leads to a stronger brand identity for that service provider. In addition, this example also raises the important issue of the advantage the stylist has as a result of the repeat business this customer provides, which naturally ties into the deep understanding of this consumer's particular preferences (i.e., This stylist knows exactly what the customer wants and can continue to deliver just that, while with other stylists the customer must explain what they want, and this often gets misinterpreted, which is why consumers tend to be very loyal to their stylists).

Because services, by definition, are intangible and cannot be held, examined, and scrutinized by the customer as products can, this raises the issue of how brand focus is altered with respect to the channel. In effect, the delivery of the service to a customer takes place as it does for a product, through both communication and distribution channels, but the distribution channel of a service is unique with respect to another difference between services and products, and that is the issue—perishability. Products can be stored in a warehouse, maintained over time, and shipped from middleman to another, but a service is delivered simultaneously to its consumption, like a doctor performing an exam, or an airline that flies a person from one city to another. In the case of both of these examples, the strategic brand focus will be impacted by these unique characteristics of a service. Some recent changes in the restaurant delivery industry offers a glimpse into the importance that the channel serves to define a company brand.

For example, the very successful startup Grubhub, which delivers food from a variety of restaurants to customers' place of residence, operates on the basis of new technology that allows someone to put an application onto their mobile phone to order food in a very convenient manner. The same is true for the delivery of transportation services like Uber or Lyft, each of which operates on the same basis where an app serves as the key link in the distribution channel. As the number of distribution channels of services, whether restaurant or transportation, increases, it provides an opportunity for the company in question to reinforce their brand in the minds of customers and potential customers. One has to assume that more positive emotional connections accrue as a company increases the size of the market base, assuming of course that there is satisfaction with the service as it is used.

CONCLUSION

Today's customer has a vast array of choices, which when combined with the fact that there are low barriers to change preferred brands makes the competitive situation more complex and uncertain.[39] The marketing industry today faces extremely rapid changes as a result of the use of technological advances that have enabled customers to seek out more personalization, with the net result of a stronger emotional connection to brands. Furthermore, the modern digital outreach has switched to "real-time" targeting as a result of the use of analytics that makes it possible for companies to track the movement of customers when they are online. Modern marketers know that the customer is no longer a passive recipient of product information, but on the contrary, is an active co-creator who shapes companies and their offerings. Therefore, to stay relevant and deliver a competitive advantage, companies need to engage in a conversation with their customers that is based on attractive narratives. In the services sector, there is more opportunity for organizations to keep that conversation alive with their customers. Transparency and the tremendously fast speed of information in today's world are some of the factors that have shaped service brands and left companies with no choice but to alter their branding strategies to center them around the needs and wants of their customers.[40]

Brand personality is crucial to effectively communicate service brand values and impact consumer perceptions. Brand personality should be developed and aligned across key dimensions including brand name, core product/service, feeling and experiences, price, user imagery, and communications and advertising to develop a strong service brand. These factors influence both B2B (business-to-business) brands as well as B2C (business-to-consumer) brands because they essentially shape the key message of the brand. A brand personality that ingrains trust and positive experience drives success for a service brand. Because word of mouth is an increasingly powerful influencing factor, amplified by social media channels and increased communication, it is more important than ever for brands to personify trust to cultivate meaningful relationships and interactions with consumers. This creates a mutually beneficial relationship, one that aids the brand's goals, as well as meets the consumers' needs in order to develop loyalty and long-lasting relationships.

George and Berry defined the most successful practices for advertising of services.[41] The six guidelines presented by the authors are as follows: Advertising to employees; capitalizing on the use of word of mouth; providing tangible clues; making the service understood; promoting continuity; and promising what is possible. Each of these areas further seeks to compensate for the possibility that unlike products which tend to be more consistent, there could be a lack of consistency across service providers, all of whom may work for the same organization. Berry believes that in service marketing, unlike goods businesses that sell tangible products, service businesses sell performance.[42] He identified seven major factors that help a service brand be successful: Distinguish between the marketing department and the marketing function; leverage the freedom factor; market to employees; market to existing customers; be great at problem resolution; think high tech and high touch; and be a power brander.

Service branding requires specific nuances to its brand strategy that vary from traditional product branding, given their unique nature in terms of consumption and customer focus. Because services are immediately consumed, rather than having the ability to be preserved, their "shelf life" varies from a traditional tangible good. Similarly, customer focus is a key component of service branding given the intimate relationship and elevated consumer expectations of consuming a service as opposed to a product. Many brands differentiate themselves on the basis of customer service levels. Moreover, service brands have unique risk exposure that must be taken into account when developing a brand strategy because of their customer service and its relationship to brand success. Given the innate variation in experiences services offer as opposed to the relatively standardized experience packaged goods offer, there is greater opportunity for experiences to differ among individuals, and potentially amplify the negative service encounters consumers have with a brand. It is increasingly more important for brands to hold positive reputations and therefore increasingly detrimental to brands who fail to pay attention to this.

Endnotes

1. Fisk, Brown and Bitner, 1993.
2. Vargo and Lusch, Evolving to a new dominant logic for marketing, 2004.
3. Ballantyne and Aitken, 2007.
4. J. C. Davis, 2007.
5. L. L. Berry, Cultivating service brand equity, 2000.
6. Berry, Lefkowith and Clark, In services, what's in a name, 1988.
7. J. C. Davis, 2007.
8. Hollis, 2014.

9. Ballantyne and Aitken, 2007.
10. Booms and Bitner, 1981.
11. Warc briefing: Service brands, 2010.
12. Charlene, 2007.
13. Ballantyne and Aitken, 2007.
14. Hollis, 2014.
15. de Chernatony and Riley, Experts' views about defining services brands and the principles of services branding, 1999.
16. de Chernatony and Segal-Horn, Building on services' characteristics to develop successful services brands, 2001.
17. Hollis, 2014.
18. Hollis, 2014.
19. Charlene, 2007.
20. Hollis, 2014.
21. Hollis, 2014.
22. L. L. Berry, Cultivating service brand equity, 2000.
23. Grace and O'Cass, 2005.
24. K. L. Keller, 1998.
25. L. L. Berry, Cultivating service brand equity, 2000.
26. Dou and Krishnamurthy, Using brand websites to build brands online: a product versus service brand comparison, 2007.
27. Mattila, 2000.
28. Lovelock and Wright, 1999.
29. Dou and Krishnamurthy, Using brand websites to build brands online: a product versus service brand comparison, 2007.
30. Davis, Buchanan-Oliver and Brodie, 2000.
31. Zuckerberg, 2016.
32. Dall'Olmo and de Chernatony, 2000.
33. Newman, The Handbook of Political Marketing, 1999.
34. Newman, The Marketing Revolution in Politics: What Recent U.S. Presidential Campaigns Can Teach Us About Effective Marketing, 2016.
35. Newman, The Marketing of the President, 1994.
36. Solomon, 2015.
37. Cieslak, 2016.
38. Arruda, 2014.
39. Tyrrell and Westall, 1998.
40. Warc briefing: Service brands, 2010.
41. George and Berry, 1981.
42. L. Berry, 1986.

CHAPTER 4

BRANDING PEOPLE

INTRODUCTION

Modern branding is not limited to products or services, but is extended to people. The branding of people includes public figures (politicians, celebrities, athletes, etc.), as well as personal branding that may involve each individual who seeks to identify themselves in a unique manner.[1] The argument put forward in this area of branding is that human personalities are consistent yet, at the same time, dynamic, and therefore a branding strategy for a person must remain clear and consistent. According to Thomson, "when a human brand enhances a person's feelings of autonomy and relatedness and does not suppress feelings of competence, the person is likely to become more strongly attached to it."[2] One of the central purposes and conclusions from his research centers on the determination of why and how consumers form strong attachments to human brands. He stated that the term "human brand" refers to any well-known persona who is the subject of marketing communications effort.

THE ROLE OF ARCHETYPES

According to Tsai, the branding of humans has a powerful archetypal component at heart.[3] The power of archetypes is derived from the human ability to identify themselves with desirable characters. Or put another way, an archetype can serve as a universal symbol, which can be identified as a character or even a symbol. In other words,

FIGURE 4.1   Strategic Brand Focus

if marketers can tap into the psyche of the customer, they can build a brand loyalty beyond rational considerations.

The theory of archetypes was introduced by Jung, who emphasized that human beings across nations and cultures share the same archetypal images, such as an image of a hero.[4] Our affinity toward and preference of certain public figures (actors, politicians, sports figures, singers, etc.) potentially help us construct our own "self, social and cultural identity."[5] Marketers can then use the power of archetypes to develop strong human brands. Strong human brands are those that tap into the psychology of the customer and the values of that person.

For example, there is the case of the "hero" figure in sports who lifts his or her team to victory against all odds. One would have to certainly attribute that branding strategy to the New England Patriots in their 2017 Super Bowl victory when Tom Brady pulled off what some have said is the biggest upset victory in sports with the come-from-behind win over the Atlanta Falcons. One can also go back to the Chicago Bulls who were lifted to stardom when Michael Jordan led them to multiple national championships. The Bulls brand acquired a status that perhaps no other team has on the back of the unbelievable feats of one person, namely Michael Jordan. On the corporate side, many have attributed a cult-like status to the Apple Corporation as a result of the "creative" genius of their CEO, Steven Jobs. Each of these examples demonstrate that potential strength can be attached to an organization, or to a person individually because of the sheer power of the archetype a person represents.

PERSONAL BRANDING

This category of branding also pertains to average individuals who seek to promote their own personal brand among others for either personal or professional gain. According to Lair, Sullivan, and Cheney, people try to adjust their images to create a desired perception in the target audience (whether in voters, employers, friends, etc.).[6] The approach can yield fruit if used with wisdom. However, in its extreme form, people strive to accommodate the needs of the market without a deep understanding of their own unique capabilities and relationships.[7] Personal branding is embedded in the American value system, which purports that a person can "create and recreate" him or herself to achieve their desired goals and dreams.[8] Since personal branding is extremely popular, various scholars have tried to explore the phenomenon and understand its roots and implications. According to Rampersad, all of us have personal brands.[9] Our behaviors, ideas, emotional responses, etc., leave a unique impression in the minds of people who know us. Unfortunately, not all people understand the importance of strategically managing their personal brands to achieve their goals and dreams. He argues that a strong personal brand is built on authenticity, which means that it reflects the true character and real actions of a person. Moreover, an authentic personal brand should motivate a person to deliver on his/her promises and be honest and true to his/her values. A powerful personal brand emerges from one's "search for identity and meaning" in life.[10]

Brennan and Mattice argue that personal branding is effective because it helps build trust in other people.[11] To establish trust, a person needs to manage all facets of the personal brand. First, the authors suggest that self-reflection and constant learning are essential for a strong personal brand. Second, strong mission and vision help develop credibility and establish direction. Finally, building and nurturing a relationships network is also crucial. The personal branding of an individual must also take into account their gender, and the impact that may have on their position within an organization. In research carried out in this area by Brescoll and Uhlmann, and Brescoll, Uhlmann, and Newman there is evidence that a person's gender does matter, and in fact can play a role in how others perceive them.[12, 13]

Despite the proven positive effects of personal branding, some scholars and practitioners believe that the phenomenon of personal branding has negative implications. For example, Lair et al. argue that personal branding could create a serious threat at work if it is not carried off in the correct manner. The authors defined personal branding as "an extreme form of market-appropriate response."[14] As we know, many different people in society try to adjust their images to meet the needs of the market when responding to a constituency of people, whether it be voters, employers, friends, or whomever. According to Lair et al., the credibility of a person, product, or service today is just an idea that is appealing at a particular moment. However, when something changes the equilibrium (a scandal, change in trends or style, etc.), the person, product, or service is no longer credible. We have seen this happen with CEO's who get into trouble with the law (like Martha Stewart) as well as Hollywood stars who wind up on the front page of magazines and newspapers that offer accounts of personal affairs that are seen as crooked or in bad taste.

CELEBRITY BRANDING, ATTACHMENT, AND ENDORSEMENT

The success of a celebrity is very much a function of the strong attachment that the public has toward that particular person. Therefore, companies in the entertainment industry, as well as politics attempt to establish strong emotional connections between their fans/supporters and the human brand, which is the Hollywood star or politician. According to Thomson, relationships between celebrities and their fans are similar to relationships that are created between any two people.[15] According to his research, emotions that are created in an individual are no different for another person or a celebrity. He also suggests that the most successful celebrity brands are those that make a person feel independent and competent.[16]

The phenomenon of celebrity worship and celebrity brand extension has been studied extensively.[17] According to the authors, marketers often use celebrity endorsements to promote their products. Going back to 2009, celebrities appeared in "about 20 percent of advertisements in the United States."[18] It is quite likely that this figure has increased since then with the increased use of it by more and more companies. It is important to mention that there exists a significant difference between a celebrity brand and an endorsed brand. A celebrity brand is a brand created and marketed by a celebrity, whereas an endorsed brand is a brand merely promoted by a chosen celebrity.[19] For example, Wolfgang Puck, a world-renowned chef, created a line of cookware and packaged foods and sauces under the Wolfgang Puck label. His brand is a celebrity brand, as Puck is involved in the product development stages as well as on the marketing side to sell his product. On the other hand, Giada De Laurentis, another celebrity chef specializing in Italian cuisine, was used to endorse Target's generic brand of pasta sauce. In Giada's case, her involvement with Target's pasta sauce was merely an endorsement, as she was engaged solely as a marketing ploy as opposed to involved throughout the creation of the actual product. Celebrity brand extensions can help create longevity and generate revenues for the celebrity. However, to be successful, celebrity brand extension should represent a "good fit" to the celebrity brand. As we see with Wolfgang Puck, his varied line of products support his brand because he sells products related to cooking. His product line is successful because he has established a brand for himself in the celebrity chef world, and therefore cooking related products are a good fit given his respected reputation as a chef.

Through the process of carrying out a strategic brand focus, and beginning with a profile of who the customer is that an organization is targeting, specific needs and wants can be identified, allowing marketers to increase the effectiveness of their campaigns by finding "the right" celebrity for each segment.[20] Moreover, the authors suggest that celebrity worship may influence the relationships between the perceived fit and consumers' attitudes toward celebrity-branded products. Interestingly enough, in certain cases of extreme celebrity worship, brand extensions weaken loyalty toward the brand as the fans can develop a negative attitude toward the commercialization of their favorite celebrity.[21] One could argue that this has taken place over the years with celebrities who appear to be constantly promoting products, services, and companies. This issue adds a certain level of complexity as one compares this type of branding to either product or service branding where such a phenomenon is not possible. It therefore highlights the importance of examining the extent to which a celebrity is involved in advertising or promoting other brands when selecting a celebrity persona to endorse a brand or product.

According to Pringle and Binet, advertising campaigns featuring celebrities do not necessarily have a significant advantage over ad campaigns that use other advertising techniques (e.g., comparative ads or humor).[22] Oftentimes advertising failures can be attributed to incorrectly selecting or executing the celebrity endorsement of the brand. What helps companies choose the right celebrity? According to the authors, the fit of a celebrity and the advertised brand; a specific brand image that the celebrity holds; areas of the celebrity's involvement with the brand; and the amount of investment in a celebrity campaign are determining factors for choosing a celebrity for an ad campaign.

According to Ilicic and Webster, celebrity endorsements help differentiate a product in a competitive marketspace.[23] In some cases, the brand image of a celebrity can affect the endorsed brand by creating associations in the customer's mind.[24, 25] Moreover, these authors point out that the endorsed product can also influence the brand image of the endorser. An alignment between the celebrity and the endorsed product are crucial for success of an ad campaign. Although creating a brand closely aligned with a celebrity can create an emotional connection or sense of inspiration that drives brand loyalty and purchase behavior, brands must also weigh the risk of placing a brand's values, capital, and personality in one person. As Behr and Beeler-Norrholm highlight, celebrity endorsements are not always a safe way to brand products because celebrities often engage in controversial activities that receive publicity which may be negative in the minds of the public.[26] Ryan Lochte, a celebrated swimmer on the American Olympic team, had a very successful 2016 Olympics in Rio and was the face of many athletic brands. However, he caused an international scandal when he was caught on film intoxicated, destroying public property, and lying about being a victim of a robbery during the Rio Olympics. As a result, his endorsement deals were terminated by high profile athletic brands, including Speedo, given that the brands did not want to be associated with his inappropriate conduct. Furthermore, in an age where stories about people can go viral in a matter of minutes, it becomes difficult to both monitor and correct this when it happens. As we saw in Lochte's example, word of his scandal spread internationally incredibly quickly and created a media frenzy fueled by the video footage that fueled discussion about his behavior. This is further indication of the additional issues that arise as one moves from product and service branding to person branding.

CELEBRITY WORSHIP

The discipline that has devoted the most attention to the subject of celebrity worship, or the obsession people have with a particular star, such as George Clooney in Hollywood, or Michael Jordan in the sports world, can be found in the psychology literature, with special attention paid to an individual's obsession with a person in the public eye.[27] Customers' attachment to the celebrity, as well as the connection between the celebrity and the product are important factors for celebrity brands. Results of work carried out in this area suggest that the level of celebrity worship may influence the relationships between perceived fit and consumers' attitudes toward celebrity-branded products. For both product types investigated in the study (clothes and weight loss products), the direct relationship between perceived fit and attitudes toward the celebrity-branded products was strong. The managerial implications to this situation suggest the following strategic considerations:

▶ Companies are encouraged to seek out celebrities to develop specific celebrity-licensing relationships that have significant profit potential for both parties.

▶ Development of celebrity brand extensions, as opposed to simple endorsement deals, can shift the risk from the company/product to the celebrities.

▶ The continued use of a particular celebrity may be extended through the branding and brand extension process.

▶ Identifying celebrities with a strong consumer attachment would allow marketers to better target their marketing efforts by using the most "fitting" celebrity for each segment.

▶ With the growth in social networks, such as Facebook and Twitter, celebrities are able to extend their brands to their fan base.

Kowalczyk and Royne make the point that there has been a blurring between the celebrity and the product they are endorsing when the celebrities themselves are no longer just endorsing products but are becoming brands themselves.[28] For example, the success of the Cleveland Cavaliers on the back of their star player, LeBron James, represents such a phenomenon where any product he endorses may be subsumed in the mind of the consumer by the sheer fan worship for him as a superstar. In effect, many would argue that LeBron, himself, has become a brand. Success of the product generally depends on the "right fit" with the celebrity. Along this line of thinking, work carried out on the relationship between negative brand publicity and a celebrity endorser poses some interesting considerations. According to the authors, such qualities allow a celebrity to play a central role in making an ad noticeable, distinctive, and memorable. At the same time, a negative image of an endorsing celebrity can damage the brand he/she endorses.

Previous studies have suggested that the relationship between negative celebrity information and brand evaluation can be moderated by certain factors.[29] These factors include, among others, consumers' brand commitment, as well as their identification with the celebrity endorsers themselves. According to Um, prior research has found that negative brand publicity lowers brand evaluation and decreases purchase intention, and for those customers forming judgments, negative information carries greater weight than positive information.[30]

SOCIAL COGNITIVE THEORY

Bandura's social cognitive theory posits that a person's identification with a model regulates the likelihood of enacting a behavior.[31]When individuals perceive themselves as similar to a model, they are more likely to enact whatever behavior that person models—an act that expresses such identification.[32] According to the author, one common proposition made by these theories is that identification is an important factor underlying attitude and behavior change. Another perspective on the identification process can be derived from something called a "para-social relationship." A para-social relationship, according to Horton and Wohl, is when an individual develops, via the media, a sense of intimacy and identification with a celebrity, which is the result of the power of the media to serve in a reinforcing capacity for those who believe what is being communicated.[33]

According to Um, "identification level with a celebrity seems to moderate the relationship between negative information and brand evaluation.[34] The more consumers identify with a celebrity, the less likely will negative press sway them." Therefore, we can conclude that a consumer's identification with a celebrity endorser is an important predictor of the brand evaluation and purchase intention. The study reinforces the notion that negative brand publicity lowers brand evaluation and decreases purchase intention. Negative information may be considered more impactful and thus given greater weight in consumer decisions.

It is clear that there are both benefits and risks associated with celebrity branding, which is certainly one of the more important areas of research in person branding. Unlike the tangible nature of a product which is much more predictable, person branding carries with it a level of risk that can either be very positively or very negatively perceived by consumers. Whereas the use of person branding for products, services, and organizations is a common occurrence, our discussion now moves to politics, where one could argue that person branding is at the heart of the success of any political organization, movement, or even nation.

BRANDING POLITICIANS

Reeves, de Chernatony, and Carrigan argue that branding in politics has become essential in capitalist societies.[35] As evidenced by the observable shift in political marketing campaigns, modern politicians are becoming more and more driven by branding.[36]

Modern politicians in developed countries use marketing strategies to better address the needs of their electorate. Singer emphasizes that a "brand promise" (or in other words, the issues and policies a candidate for office promises to pursue if elected) is what differentiates one political candidate from another.[37] The subjectivity of brand images is evident in politics and political branding. Even the appearance of a politician can help or damage his/her brand image. Hoegg and Lewis argue that political candidates "are at an advantage when there is a match between personality traits inferred from their physical appearance and the traits associated with their party."[38] The 2016 U.S. presidential campaign exemplifies the need to align public appearance with party values to create a cohesive brand. Bernie Sanders campaigned heavily on the platform of creating a political system that benefits all American citizens, as opposed to the "top 1%." His public appearances supported this stance, as he projected a cost-conscious image: He opted to fly coach as opposed to private planes commonly used by candidates; did not dress ostentatiously; and kept frivolous expenses to a minimum. Contrasting Sander's brand with that of Donald Trump, who outwardly favored big business and unregulated capitalism, personified this stance by aligning his personal brand with wealth and luxury. Trump used private jets and flaunted luxury material items throughout his campaign. Given the stark differences in how these two candidates viewed the role of wealth in their political campaigns, each of their personal brands had to be clearly aligned with their political positions throughout the campaign.

Modern communication demands direct interaction and personalized meaning. According to Alani, social media can powerfully overcome the feeling of alienation in voters during a political campaign.[39] For example, the presence of Barack Obama on Twitter during his presidential campaigns in 2008 and 2012, and Donald Trump during the 2016 campaign, has been considered one of the most essential elements of a campaign's success.[40] According to Yan, Twitter is an "informal" engagement tool that Barack Obama and his campaign team leveraged to give Americans the opportunity to ask questions and directly engage with the candidate.[41] What began with Barack Obama in 2008 continued on to be increasingly influential in the 2016 presidential campaign, where one would have to argue that Donald Trump's election success was due in large part to his use of Twitter and both a medium to reinforce his relationship with his followers as well as to drive the agenda setting of the traditional media.

Hoegg and Lewis used a combination of laboratory studies and analysis of actual U.S. election results to explore influences of candidate appearance and spending strategies in political campaigns.[42] The authors examined how personality judgments based on candidate appearance interact with marketing variables, including party brand image, advertising spending, and negative advertising. The previous research showed that candidates with an appearance conveying a high level of overall competence enjoy greater electoral success. The authors discovered that "within the positive perceptual space related to candidates' perceived competence, there exist subtle but distinct traits that can be communicated visually and have greater explanatory power than an overall measure."[43] The authors claimed that "candidates are at an advantage when there is a match between personality traits inferred from their physical appearance and the traits associated with their party." The authors found that effects of physical appearance at the candidate level to be dependent on trait associations at the party level.

It is widely accepted that candidate appearance influences election results, and prior work has considered many elements such as height, hair, and attractiveness.[44] The results suggest that appearance should be evaluated in concert with party affiliation, in terms of candidate selection, and even in terms of managing candidate appearance. According to the authors, given the role of a brand's personality in developing customer loyalty, the potential interaction between visually inferred personality traits and brand-level personality traits is an important topic for further research.

THE ROLE OF NEGATIVE ADVERTISING IN BRANDING POLITICIANS

During elections, politicians increasingly count on negative advertising in their political campaigns. In some cases, negative ads are effective, as they "reduce target-candidate support."[45] In other situations, negative political ads produce the "boomerang effects," and cause an unintentional increase of the opponent's supporters. For example, when Jimmy Carter attacked Ronald Reagan with a negative attack against him because of his age, Reagan was able to present himself as a lucid thinker, quick on his feet, and this negative attack ultimately hurt Carter because it was not seen as believable. According to other researchers, the favorability status of a candidate is a determining factor when deciding whether or not to use negative ads. Friestad and Wright connected poll results and candidate status to study the interactive relationships between poll standing and negative advertising use.[46] According to their results, negative advertising created a more positive response among consumers when used by politicians who were ahead in the polls than when negative advertising was used by their challengers who were further behind in the polls. They also point out that voters tend to understand the hidden agenda behind negative ads, and they tend to disbelief them, resulting oftentimes in those kinds of advertisements not being very effective.

Keith Coulter helps us further explore the topic of negative political advertising. As the author argues, negative advertising is more memorable, and has profound effect on voters' attitudes and perceptions.[47] However, to accurately evaluate the amount of negative political advertising, researchers still have to find consensus on the definition of negative advertising in politics. Some researchers identify negative political ads as the ads that contain "disapproving statements" about a political opponent. Other researchers believe that it is necessary to differentiate between those advertisements that are negative in nature and those that are labeled as "attack ads." He argues that negative ads can be divided into three categories, "direct attack, direct comparison, and implied comparison":

- ▶ Direct attack ads are primarily focused on disparaging the competitor;
- ▶ Direct comparison ads compare a candidate to his/her opponent on several characteristics to directly convey the sponsor's positive traits;
- ▶ Implied comparison ads show the differences between candidates in an implicit manner so that voters are prompted to make their own assumptions.

Coulter claims that in spite of the U.S. democratic values, negative political advertising in America is surprisingly prevalent. Political candidates tend to use negative advertising as a "righteous" representation of their competitors' flaws, and their own benefits. The prevalence exists because negative advertising is a tactic that works. He points out that while negative product advertising differentiates a product based on a physical quality, negative political marketing separates one candidate from another based on a dimension of personality and policy differences. Therefore, one negative political ad may produce different effects in different groups of voters based on their initial attitudes toward the candidate using the negative ads. This raises a question with respect to the type of negative political advertising that works the best and why.

Wood explored the practical application of negative political advertising. According to the author, negative advertising predominates in the U.S. political arena.[48] Negative advertising produces more news and tends to be very high-profile. However, negative political advertising can bring both positive and negative publicity for the ad sponsor. Furthermore, the author argues that negative political advertising may produce negative attitudes about candidates in both parties at the same time. Negative advertising can also produce different effects on various groups of voters. Gianatasio explored effective social media tools that marketing and political campaigns used to reach millennials.[49] The author makes the point that millennials are considered to be a hard-to-reach audience, and content and platform are the two most important factors to get a political message across to them. He suggests that politicians should rely on political content that is sincere and supported by facts since millennials actively use research tools to verify.

The research in this area raises another very important distinction that comes with person branding, and that is the ability to use person branding to carry out a negative campaign in the most effective manner possible. It is easier for a person to voice an opinion about another company or person, or in this current illustration, another politician, than it is for an organization that sells a product or service to attack another organization. Each person, whether it is a celebrity endorsing a politician, or a politician themselves attacking another one, has the right to state their opinion. Thus, from a strategic standpoint, this is a unique consideration political branding carries that must be taken into account for all types of person branding.

CASE STUDIES OF PERSON BRANDING

Case 1: Branding the Pope

One human brand that has captured the hearts and minds of people around the world is Pope Francis. As is usually the case, a company's leader often personifies its brand. The mission of the Catholic Church is more important than that of an ordinary organization and the Pope represents more than just a brand. One of the unique characteristics of the Pope's brand identity is that he is perceived as a genuinely humble person. This is unlike what many people would assume comes with the power of his position. In fact, many would assume that the Pope would take full advantage of his position of privilege. But this is quite contrary to his decision not to live in the same part of the Vatican that his predecessors did, but instead, live in a simple room with other religious leaders around him. Perhaps it is this humility that successfully brands this religious leader, as he is someone who is able to communicate to many different people in a very effective manner. This is also accomplished through many different channels, as it is well known that the Pope uses the Internet and various social media outlets extensively. Through his chosen lifestyle, the Pope creates a perception of authenticity and altruism, which has in turn led to widespread public support that transcends both religion and culture.[50]

Case 2: Branding Donald Trump

Throughout the campaign, Mr. Trump built up his brand by crafting his image as a nonpolitician who would fix the economic and foreign policy problems afflicting the country, relying on Twitter and Facebook to connect with over 25 million citizens. As the technological breakthroughs in business continue to be transplanted in the political marketplace, dramatic changes can be seen in how U.S. citizens choose their presidential candidates, and is responsible for the beginning stages of a paradigm shift in electoral politics that has moved control from the political party to micro-campaigns. This has provided the opportunity for nonpoliticians like Mr. Trump to circumvent the traditional political distribution channel and rise to the top of the ticket without getting the nod of party insiders, in the same way that Uber and Airbnb have done it in the ride-sharing and apartment rental markets. A direct distribution channel between presidential candidates and citizens now exists, and will shape future presidential campaigns through a reliance on Big Data, Social Media, and Micro-targeting.[51]

At the end of the 2016 U.S. Presidential Election, one would have to argue that Donald Trump did to his brand what every person or organization has to do to successfully compete in any marketplace, and that is to create a narrative around their brand. In 2016, Trump represented the most attractive brand possible as the consummate outsider who appealed to those voters who lost their trust in Washington leaders. In addition to that, his brand as a businessman allowed him a great deal of latitude to say and do things as a political candidate that most other presidential contenders could not get away with. For example, he was excused from having to live up to a level of decency in his behavior that other more traditional politicians were not excused from. Many of the indecencies that he exhibited during the campaign were not taken as seriously, because business leaders are not held up to the same level of scrutiny as politicians are.

The Clinton brand was heavily tarnished from the e-mail scandal; speaking for hundreds of thousands of dollars; and her perception as a dishonest politician. In people marketing there must be a strong connection between the message and the messenger, which Trump had, which was a strong, confident politician promising to "Make America Great Again" (a very effective campaign slogan helping to build up his brand) and his targeted message of bringing back more jobs to America through trade deals and the threat of kicking out immigrants who took the jobs of blue-collar workers who were looking for a solution to their economic problems. Clinton's constant hammering away at Trump's tarnished brand ultimately failed because voters were willing to forgive him, but not her. In the end, Trump's brand had a positive narrative and Clinton's had a negative narrative, and voters were looking for someone to follow who could connect with voters emotionally, and positive feelings work better than negative ones at the presidential level of politics in the U.S.

Marketing today is all about building a relationship with your customers, whether it is the reward cards and vouchers that bring you back to the same retailers, airlines, or any other business that successfully convinces its customers to stick with them and not switch to the competition. Voters who supported Trump were constantly rein-forced with his use of Twitter in particular, and solidified his base, something that Clinton did not do as effectively, which was partly due to her failure in the campaign. Furthermore, Trump was successful in getting enough voters who had cast a ballot for Obama in 2012 to switch over to him instead of going with the "standard-bearer" of the Democratic Party, Hillary Clinton.

STRATEGIC BRAND FOCUS

From a strategic point of view, the question that arises is the comparative role that branding plays when it comes to people branding with respect to the discussion thus far in the book on the branding of products and services. If we go back to Figure 1.1, and examine the 3 C's, it will become clear how people branding stands out as unique from the branding of products and services, and why there are unique characteristics that are attached to this kind of branding that make the challenge slightly more com-plex and difficult for a marketer.

First of all, the customer who is targeted in a branding campaign driven by a person-oriented campaign can cut across a wide array of organizations, including commer-cial, political, nonprofit, as well as individual-oriented campaigns driven by people, such as those who seek to drive their thinking or personal brand over social media. In addition to the fact that this type of branding is highly variable due to the fact that it is person-driven, there is a risk of tremendous failure if the person in question does not live up to their archetypal reputation (such as Hillary Clinton in the 2016 U.S. Presidential election, where her supporters saw her as a "hero" figure to women who saw her as breaking through barriers as the first female presidential nominee of one of the two major parties).

Secondly, there are issues that tie into the channel strategy for this kind of branding. It is important for human brands to be highly visual, and therefore channels like tele-vision and in-person appearances are often required, which often drive up the cost of the whole marketing campaign. Selling a product can be done very effectively through mediums that do not call for the use of television, where an image of a package or design of a product can be easily conveyed through other mediums like print, online, and other less costly channels. It is therefore important to consider the cost-benefit tradeoff when leveraging human brands and selecting the appropriate channel strategy.

Third, there is the critical importance that is tied into the emotional connection that the human brand can create, and therefore the careful development of attitudes and intentions as part of a human branding strategy become more important than would be for a product. On the other hand, the strong emotional component that comes with person branding offers an opportunity to the organization that is relying on that as the focus of their strategic focus, thus increasing the likelihood that the connection between customer and organization behind the person being branded will stay intact and not as easily switched to another organization if there is a strong archetype used. For example, during the reign of Michael Jordan, there was not really any other basketball star that could have created the same level of loyalty to a basketball team as the Bulls were able to do with their fans.

CONCLUSION

When using people as a branding tool, either in the form of personal branding, celebrity branding/endorsements, or political branding, it is important to note the nuances the human element brings to developing a brand strategy. Ensuring a good fit between human branding/celebrity endorsement and the consumer is a critical first step in developing human brand strategy. The individual representing the brand, company, product, or service must align with the target consumer audience. That is, careful analysis of the target consumer audience must be conducted in tandem with selection of the individual to represent the brand in order to ensure this person can effectively address and represent a specific audience. A good fit drives purchase behavior and brand loyalty, and hence the brand must ensure the person they select embodies or closely mirrors the values, desires, and characteristics of their ideal consumer. Part of what determines what a good fit would look like comes from the Social Cognitive Theory developed by sociologist Albert Bandura in the 1980s. Essentially, when consumers view similarities between themselves and a human brand, they are likely to behave the way the individual in the human brand does—hence the effectiveness of celebrity endorsements and brands. When used appropriately, consumers mirror the desired behavior (i.e., purchasing, brand loyalty, etc.) portrayed by the individual representing the brand.

The branding of politicians is a fundamental part of the ever-evolving political landscape. A politician's brand must align with the values of their consumers, or the general public whose vote in which the politician is trying to earn. The politician must focus on relationship building in order to better understand the struggles and key issues of the population, as well as effectively market themselves as a superior candidate than other political competitors in addressing and resolving these issues. Additionally, candidates are measured not only on the relationships they form, but how much they align with a certain political look. There is increasing pressure to have an appearance of strong leadership, encompassing aspects of general physical attractiveness and appearance, dress and style, public speaking, and observable interpersonal communication. As we've seen in modern political campaigns, the use of negative advertising is widely employed by candidates, and aims to tarnish the brand of competing candidates by illuminating unfavorable actions or aspects of their opponents.

In the digital age, public figures often need to communicate with highly diverse audiences that decode and interpret information in different ways. According to Kaplan and Haenlein, branders should carefully choose social media channels, and ensure that their activities are aligned with the brand.[52] Moreover, honesty and personal approach are crucial in the cluttered online space. As the role of social media is fast becoming a critical channel of communication among and between people, the uniqueness of person branding will be that much more difficult to control when compared to product and service branding where the interpretation of the narrative being used to define the brand is less open to interpretation. This will call for more monitoring on the part of person branders to ensure that the intended narrative and identity of a person is perceived along the lines that were intended by the sender.

Endnotes

1. Bendisch, Larsen and Trueman, 2007.
2. Thomson, 2006.
3. Tsai, 2006.
4. Jung, The Archetypes and the Collective Unconscious, 1938.
5. Tsai, 2006.
6. Lair, Sullivan and Cheney n.d.
7. Phillipson, 2002.
8. Lair, Sullivan and Cheney n.d.
9. Rampersad, 2010.
10. Rampersad, 2010.
11. Brennan and Mattice, 2014.
12. Brescoll and Uhlmann, Can an angry woman get ahead? Gender, status conferral, and workplace emotion expression, 2008.
13. Brescoll, Uhlmann, and Newman, The effects of system-justifying motivations on endorsement of essentialist explanations for gender differences, 2013.
14. Lair, Sullivan and Cheney n.d.
15. Thomson, 2006.

16. Thomson, 2006.
17. Kowalczyk and Royne, 2013.
18. Solomon, 2009.
19. Kowalczyk and Royne, 2013.
20. Kowalczyk and Royne, 2013.
21. Kowalczyk and Royne, 2013.
22. Pringle and Binet, 2005.
23. Ilicic and Webster, Effects of multiple endorsements and consumer–celebrity attachment on attitude and purchase intention, 2011.
24. McCracken, 1989.
25. Ilicic and Webster, Effects of multiple endorsements and consumer–celebrity attachment on attitude and purchase intention, 2011.
26. Behr and Beeler-Norrholm, 2006.
27. McCutcheon and Lange, 2002.
28. Kowalczyk and Royne, 2013.
29. Edwards and La Ferle, 2009.
30. Um, 2013.
31. Bandura, 1986.
32. Um, 2013.
33. Horton and Wohl, 1956.
34. Um, 2013.
35. Reeves, de Chernatony, and Carrigan, 2006.
36. Newman, 2016.
37. Singer, 2002.
38. Hoegg and Lewis, 2011.
39. Alani, 2010.
40. Newman, 2016.
41. Yan, 2011.
42. Hoegg and Lewis, 2011.
43. Hoegg and Lewis, 2011.
44. Leigh and Susilo, 2009.
45. Chou and Lien, 2010.
46. Friestad and Wright, 1994.
47. Coulter, 2008.
48. Wood, 2003.
49. Gianatasio, 2014.
50. Hagenbuch, 2016.
51. Newman, 2016.
52. Kaplan and Haenlein, 2010.

CHAPTER 5

BRANDING OF ORGANIZATIONS

INTRODUCTION

This chapter will address the branding of organizations which have been broken down into three different categories: corporations, nonprofits, and political organizations. Each of these different types of organizations are all engaged in branding activities that centers on the conclusion drawn in earlier chapters on the branding of products, services, and people.

At a high level, corporations selling products or services to a wide range of customers will need to incorporate different branding strategies for each of their products and/ or services, but will also need to establish a brand identity for the corporation that identifies what it stands for in the minds of customers, regardless of the breadth and depth of the goods it sells. Take the BMW corporation for example, a company that sells several different types of automobiles, including sedans, SUV's, vans, and other types of vehicles. In addition to establishing a unique brand image for each of the line of cars they sell, BMW must successfully establish a brand identity that corresponds to the corporation as a whole, which many would argue is one of high quality, durability, and safety, based on good engineering over many years. As long as each of their new model automobiles continue to live up to the BMW brand reputation, the company will continue to excel in the marketplace.

This raises two key issues with respect to the branding corporations as compared to the branding of products, services, or people. Firstly, the brand reputation of a corporation

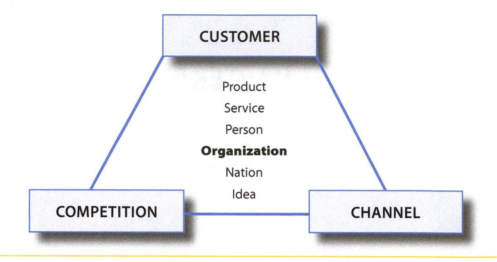

FIGURE 5.1   Strategic Brand Focus

hinges primarily on the success of their products and services. In the case of a corporation that sells a product that fails, such as classic cases like the 1957 Edsel with Ford; or the 1985 New Coke; or the 1990 Coors Rocky Mountain Spring Water; or the 1993 Apple Newton; or the 2006 Mobile ESPN; or the 2011 HP Touchpad, the brand reputation of the company will be diminished, in some cases over a period of time, but usually is only a temporary setback for the company. Secondly, there are the cases of a corporation's CEO getting into legal trouble, such as Martha Stewart, thereby creating problems for her corporation, Martha Stewart Living Omnimedia, or CEO's who are fired or pass away, creating conflicts for succession. In any one of these cases, the point is that organization branding is not only subject to the successes and failures of products and services the company sells, but also to the successes and failures of the people that run them, tying into the chapter on people branding. This leads to a more complex level of branding that must take into consideration additional factors that may or may not be subject to the control of the organization.

The case of a nonprofit is a slightly different case where the organization is not necessarily selling a line of goods or services, but instead is in the business of promoting a brand identity that is more closely tied into the purpose and focus of the organization, regardless of whether it is seeking donations; requesting people to engage in a specific activity, such as protecting the environment; or seeking to advocate a particular political position in society. Whereas these are not necessarily the only types of nonprofits that operate, they do represent a type of organization that sets them apart from the corporation. In fact, it is more likely that a nonprofit will be more closely connected to a particular individual who seeks to take advantage of their notoriety in society, like former president Bill Clinton, whose foundation is in the business of representing different causes. In this case, the conclusions drawn in the previous chapter on people branding will have more pertinence to the establishment of a nonprofit than the chapter on products. The chapter on services may become relevant for a nonprofit if it is in the business of carrying out services for people who can't afford to help themselves, like the homeless.

Finally, political organizations represent even another type of organization that is unique and different from corporations and nonprofits because they are in the business of running government, and as part of that service activity they are engaged in, they may need to understand the conclusions drawn in the chapter on services, as well as the chapter on people, where it becomes an imperative for a political party to have a person at the top of a ticket who can effectively brand it. Whereas a political party is clearly not seeking to sell products and services from a traditional perspective, they do in effect sell a service to citizens, and seek from them the allegiance that a nonprofit would also seek from their contributors or donors who help them stay in business. Without success at the ballot box, a political party will not have the opportunity to run government. As the chapter unfolds, the strategic focus for each type of organization will be highlighted and set apart from each of the other ones being discussed.

CORPORATIONS

Corporate branding is focused on strengthening the reputation of a company in the eye of its key stakeholders. According to Balmer and Greyser, the new area of "corporate-level" marketing has been receiving increasingly more attention of scholars and practitioners.[1] Over the past decade, corporate brands have become very strong drivers of financial value for corporations, and according to Martin Roll, CEO of Venture Republic, they have become balance sheet assets in and of themselves.[2] Who would not agree that the brand value of Starbucks is not a great asset, if not the greatest asset that Starbucks has going for it? This becomes reinforced with the fact that one could find a Starbucks restaurant in almost every major city across the U.S., as well as in many different cities around the world, including the Forbidden City in Beijing.

Many scholars consider corporate branding as the highest level of marketing.[3] It is important to note that corporate branding has several distinctions from product branding. According to Hatch and Schultz, corporate branding requires much more transparency than other types of branding, which often is due to both legal and public opinion pressures on corporations to run their companies in an open manner that allows for scrutiny on the part of both the government and public.[4] Additionally, corporate branding requires the attention of senior level managers, while product branding can be handled by general managers and marketing specialists. Finally, while product branding targets customers, corporate branding has all the key stakeholders in their focus (from customers to employees, to investors, to media, etc.).

Effective corporate branding is essential to meet the competition and continue growing.[5, 6, 7] The modern market is becoming more and more complex. According to Roll, due to tough competition in the global markets, expenses to maintain product capabilities, rising cost for R&D, and short product life cycles, managers should choose corporate branding as a long-term competitive advantage.[8] It is also important to note that corporate marketing can be applied to all types of businesses, from corporations to small businesses, to nonprofits.[9] Companies recognize their need for corporate branding as the competition becomes fiercer, and product branding continues to provide a long-term competitive advantage. Therefore, the importance of corporate branding motivates companies to spend more on corporate branding activities.

THE ROLE OF STAKEHOLDERS

At the center of corporate branding is the notion of building a long-term relationship between a company and its stakeholders.[10] Unfortunately, as often happens, the corporate vision of a company may differ from the way the company is perceived by its stakeholders (e.g., negative media coverage, employee dissatisfaction, etc.). The Nike Corporation brand suffered from negative media coverage in the 1990s as a result of the working conditions in their contract factories. Because of this, the corporate vision and views of stakeholders should convey similar ideas. As long as there exists an alignment between them, a corporation is viewed as credible and authentic.[11] Moreover, stakeholders form their perceptions with every message sent by a corporation or its constituents.[12] Hatch and Schultz argue that external and internal relationships that a company forms has merged, which unites all possible stakeholders of a company and provides communication paths between the participants that were not engaged during the early stages of business.[13]

Ultimately, corporate brands represent a set of intangible characteristics grounded in the stakeholders' mind. According to Hogl and Hupp, the company's reputation is the "ultimate intangible" in the minds of key stakeholders.[14] The authors argue that strong corporate brands thrive due to the following advantages: customer's trust for new products; corporation's attractiveness to potential human resources; attractiveness for major and small investor expectations; and predictability of future profits. The founder of Sony, Akio Morita, once said: "I have always believed that the company name is the life of an enterprise. It carries responsibility and guarantees the quality of the product."[15] Perhaps more important than any other motivating factor for the employees of any corporation is the pride they feel toward their employer, and the desire to do anything in their power to help them succeed.

MANAGEMENT'S ROLE

The importance of corporate branding is hard to overestimate. A damaged corporate name is usually detrimental for a company's success.[16] They argue that top managers frequently underestimate brand and reputation risks. Corporate brand management should be a part of the overall corporate strategy to preserve the company's greatest assets. Corporate branding is a marketing activity that strengthens the reputation of a company in the eye of its key stakeholders.

Einwiller and Will developed an integrated framework of corporate branding on the basis of an empirical study conducted among communication executives in eleven different multi-national companies.[17] According to their findings, stakeholders form their perceptions with every message sent by a corporation or its constituents. Therefore, the authors propose that corporate brands can be managed by means of "behavior, communication, and symbolism." They also make the point that corporate brands should be effectively managed given the increasing importance of capital markets. This trend creates implications, such as the increased competition for corporate recruiting of top talent as well as a growing demand for increased transparency. Traditionally, corporate communication is considered the most important facet in building a corporate brand. However, the authors argue that all dimensions of corporate behavior should be managed to convey an overall positive message, spanning from internal communications to outward communications visible by investors, consumers, and the general public. The authors determined that corporate focus has significantly switched from the public interest to financial success. Having analyzed the data received from a number of communication executives in multinational companies, the authors determined that most of their respondents ranked their financial stakeholders first followed by customers, the general public, and then the government. In other words, from a branding strategy perspective, it is in the best interest for corporations to work closely with those key opinion leaders in the financial sector that influence the reporting of information about the company.

Hatch and Schultz created a model to help managers align their strategic, organizational, and corporate cultures.[18] They believe that the modern market is becoming more and more complex, and thus effective differentiation in the market demands closer attention to the positioning of a corporation. Corporate brands help both differentiate and create loyalty among its stakeholders. In fact, corporate branding has several distinctions from product branding. While product branding targets customers, corporate branding has all the key stakeholders in focus. They argue that corporate branding requires much more organizational effort than product branding. The whole organization should be aligned to create a strong corporate brand. In order to address the need for integration, the authors created a model of corporate branding which emphasizes that the corporate brand identity is equally created by people inside the organizations, as well as by the external audiences. Their approach also emphasizes that there be an understanding of current problems, whether it is from the perspective of internal organizations' issues or problems that deal with their stakeholders to ensure that there is an alignment of the company's legacy and present situation with its future strategy and direction.

Balmer also argued that corporate branding calls for a different approach toward traditional marketing concepts and framework.[19] He suggests that business identity is an ambiguous term that can be seen from different points of view. He thinks corporate values are often vague and unclear for its constituents due to ineffective corporate branding. To eliminate the confusion, Urde proposed that any framework that focuses on building up a corporate brand should be based on core values of the organization.[20] Modern corporate branding requires a holistic approach toward the whole organization and its multiple stakeholders.

BRIDGING THE GAP BETWEEN THE BRAND AND THE ORGANIZATION

A gap exists between corporate brand identity and corporate brand reputation.[21] As it often happens, the image that an organization tries to project might not match the company's reputation, which is the set of established associations about its trustworthiness and goodness, hence, the corporation's brand building serves to bridge that gap. A good example of the "gap" is Chevron and the anti-Chevron movements that started in 2009. At that time, Chevron launched "We agree" campaign in an attempt to address controversies around its corporate brand and create awareness of environmental problems. However, Chevron encountered protests against the company with a series of parodies on Chevron's ads in the media upon the campaign launch because of the conflicting nature of a car company attempting to present itself as environmentally conservative.[22] According to Harris and de Chernatony, the goal of corporate branding is to bring about the "congruence between the values of the organization and the values of the brand."[23] In Chevron's case the mismatch between organizational values (which were not necessarily environmentally friendly) and their attempt to align brand values as environmentally friendly caused public backlash and was not an effective branding technique for the company.

According to Aaker, strong corporate brands are built on credibility in the eye of its key stakeholders.[24] Unfortunately, as it often happens, as observed in Chevron's case, corporate visions may differ from the current experiences of all types of stakeholders (e.g., negative media coverage, employee dissatisfaction, etc.). Therefore, the author insists that the corporate vision and views of stakeholders should convey similar ideas. As long as there exists an alignment between them, a corporation is viewed as credible and authentic. Therefore, corporate brands should be managed by means of "behavior, communication, and symbolism" to ensure a consistent brand messaging across various touch points.[25] Hatch and Schultz argued that in the digital era modern media unites all possible stakeholders and builds communication paths between the participants that were not previously engaged.[26, 27]

CORPORATE BRANDING ETHICS

Ethical branding refers to certain "moral rules that define right and wrong in branding decisions."[28] Ethical corporate behavior is grounded in the corporate reputation. It embraces the company's past and future, its employee relations, and other activities such as social engagement and charity activities among many others. A strong corporate brand should be legal and ethical, since the primary purpose of corporate branding is to strengthen the company's reputation and to "embody the value system."[29] Therefore, the corporate brand should be built upon a series of values that are clearly communicated at each brand touch point. TOMS Shoes exemplifies an ethical brand built upon social responsibility. TOMS Shoes has centered its purpose-driven marketing model around the life-long relationship with its customer and the community.

Their corporate values include environmental and humanitarian responsibility, which is clearly communicated through all aspects of their business model, from sustainable sourcing and manufacturing of the shoes themselves to their One to One campaign where purchases drive the donation of TOMS products to communities. Moreover, TOMS Shoes' executive team is highly visible in its efforts, the company created a Chief Giving Officer role to oversee community development, donations, and sponsorship. In all aspects of their ongoing business activities, TOMS emphasizes their value on building a better world, from transparent and ethical product development through post purchase donation processes, which ultimately values and solidifies the brand as ethical and therefore differentiated in today's market.

Fan explored the interplay between ethical branding and corporate reputation. He discovered that branding ethics is a subject that was neglected by many researchers.[30] Traditionally, brand equity is measured by the financial performance of a brand. However, this approach has certain limitations and deficiencies. The author claims that corporate branding has a powerful ethical component that reinforces loyalty and creates a positive reputation. Unfortunately, many companies successfully manipulate the consumer by marketing actions that may be considered unethical. Moreover, unethical decisions may come from activities not directly related to marketing. In this era of fast transmission of information via the Internet, brand identity can be tarnished even by a small negative event that received some media coverage. Furthermore, inspiring corporate mission statements sometimes are far from the truth. Fan argues that a corporate brand may hold multiple images, and a gap can exist between corporate goals of maximizing profits at any price, and a positive and inspiring corporate mission. Therefore, a strong corporate brand should be both legal and ethical, since the primary purpose of corporate branding is to strengthen the company's reputation.

Ethical corporate behavior is grounded in the corporate reputation. It embraces the company's past, and future, its employee relations, and other activities, such as social engagement and charity activities, to among many others.[31] Moreover, financial performance is created by the company's reputation, and at the same time, influenced by it. The author argues that a popular brand might not be ethical. Moreover, ethical behavior does not guarantee a big market share. However, as the author explained, despite conflicting findings in the literature, modern customers care more about ethical issues today than they did in decades past.

EMPLOYMENT ADVERTISING

Corporate branding is unique in that recruiting efforts are part of the brand identity. Employment advertising is one of the most visible, recognizable, and memorable elements of organizational communication, which plays a key role in the development of a company's brand identity. Traditionally, employment ads have the intention of attracting suitable applicants to vacant positions, not to build or contribute to brand equity in any direct way.[32] However, nowadays, we see recruitment messages that look and feel like brand messages. The authors emphasized that employees are being viewed as no longer a secondary audience, but a primary one. Firms such as IBM, GE, BP, Shell, and Chevron, to name a few, have been utilizing mass media techniques to reach the wider community not necessarily to sell, but to educate, inform, remind, and communicate. Employment marketing trends include:

- ► There is an ongoing struggle for talent and skill shortages, and the employment brands enable companies to attract the best candidates that they are looking for.
- ► The concept of employment brands is built on the stakeholder concept, seeing an employee as a valuable stakeholder.
- ► Successful global brands treat employees as internal customers, and positions as internal products.

Firms are facing skills shortages, and have to resort to employment branding in order to deal with these deficiencies, according to de Bussy et al.[33] The authors claim that regardless of the employment proposition/employment brand type, all advertising should attempt to differentiate the brand from direct competitors. This translates to: Stability and mobility (for well-established companies); Excitement and new experiences (for startups to create awareness and reduce psychological risks for potential employees); and Identification as a source of similarity ("Join us and succeed too" as reduction of psychological risks) are all classified as employment advertising messages used to recruit top talent.

According to the authors, being able to understand employment brand equity will be one more performance milestone that managers will have to develop a deeper understanding of, measure, and manage. The authors believe that the notion of Employment Brand Equity is a valuable component to the overall corporate brand, and will therefore need to be integrated into the overall task of stakeholder management.

HOW PORTFOLIO STRATEGIES HAVE CHANGED

The analysis of current trends in the corporate branding and brand architecture reflect a tendency of companies to move away from corporate branding in favor of mono, endorsed, dual, and mixed brands to protect their brands from a potential damage due to possible reputation risks. Laforet and Saunders suggested that brand management should be a part of the overall strategy to conserve companys' greatest assets.[34] The reputational risk is perceived by many businesses as the main potential hazard for a business. A damaged corporate name is usually detrimental for a company's success. According to the authors, "Corporate branders, like Kellogg's and Nestlé, who use their corporate names to endorse their range, face reputation risk across their whole business if bad news hits. In contrast, Unilever and Mars' use of mono brands gives firebreaks that can limit reputation loss across a whole business."[35]

Brand portfolios need to integrate top managers throughout the corporate branding process to strategically align the various parts and departments of the company as well as mitigate the risk of damaged corporate reputation.[36] According to the authors,

> "In a time of increased technological change in products and media, the brand, that apparently most ephemeral of things, is the one constant link between marketer and customer. Brands figure among the most valuable asset of a company yet recent scandals show that asset to be highly vulnerable. Reputations that take years to build can be lost in days. When brands fail, branding becomes a boardroom issue. The evidence from this audit suggests that many companies are taking those risks seriously and seeking ways of leveraging their brand equity while limiting their exposure to reputation risk."

They also believe there exists a significant change in brand strategies in the past ten years, and the authors suggested three steps to avoid threats to the corporate reputation:

1. Brands should be a board level issue and have appropriate representation.
2. To reduce the risk to the corporate reputation and to preserve strong brand identities, companies should de-capitalize by keeping the corporate name separate from individual brand. (It should be pointed out here that this thinking is contrary to some of the findings reported earlier in this section.)

3. The group of key brands needs managing and exploiting with great care. A company's lesser brands can then be mixed and matched to achieve the short-term gains so beloved of marketer.

Corporate branding is focused on strengthening the reputation of a company in the eye of stakeholders. Many scholars recognize that effective corporate branding is essential to address the competition and continue growing.[37, 38, 39] In spite of the obvious benefits, however, brand-boosting activities are often underfunded, due to the lack of attention and resources that exist when product brands have no direct connection with the corporate brand.[40] Unfortunately, there still exists confusion about corporate branding and its dimensions.[41, 42] According to Einwiller and Will, the digital age and connectivity has created a need for strong investor relations, as well as effective protection of talent in the "war for talent."[43] Moreover, the authors called for more transparency, synergy, and integration of corporate brand messages in multi-national corporations. Whereas globalization still remains a challenge for modern companies, the authors recommended that multi-national companies adopt the methods of cross-functional teams and centralized coaching to deliver consistent corporate messages across all of its constituents.

NONPROFITS

Nonprofit branding is an understudied field of marketing. Unfortunately, nonprofit marketers often apply branding frameworks from commercial branding without adjusting them, which might not be as effective as strategies individually tailored for every nonprofit. Stride and Lee explored the peculiarities of branding in the charity environment. The authors argue that nonprofit organizations can enjoy a sustained growth when they adopt some branding techniques used in the commercial sector.[44] However, the strategies should be adjusted to the charity organizations. No longer just a logo, commercial and nonprofit brands are complex psychological entities that can provide "emotional and self-expressive benefits" to the consumer. The authors support the idea that strategic branding in the nonprofit sector helps to increase an organization's presence in the mind of their target market, as well as to build loyalty with them, and ultimately to increase donations. Effective branding in the nonprofit sector is a slightly more complex endeavor than one would find in the commercial marketplace, as one needs to meet the needs of donors, in addition to influencing key entities, including commercial partners, the government, and the public. Moreover, the authors believe that trust building is one of the most important tasks for nonprofit brand managers.

Stride and Lee conducted an empirical study to conceptualize nonprofit brands. They conducted interviews with eight directors of different large nonprofit organizations, and analyzed the data using a coding system. According to the results of their study, they discovered that the interviewed executives predominantly do not perceive non-profit branding in terms of positioning and competition.[45] More often than not, the nonprofit executives talked about charity branding in terms of tangible brand image, such as the name or logo of the organization. The authors explain the results by the evidence that the communication within nonprofits is a complex task to unite multiple internal stakeholder groups, and as a result, managers tend to focus on the concrete dimensions of branding to manage the process. Furthermore, the authors argue that nonprofit brand managers need to acquire a flexible approach toward nonprofit char-ity branding, as a result of the constraints oftentimes imposed upon them by their commercial counterparts. They also recommend that brand managers first identify the values that unite the organization, and once identified, the values need to be commu-nicated to stakeholders both from within and outside the organization.

EMOTIONAL BRANDING

According to Baghi and Gabrielli, consumers are generally skeptical about for-profit organizations that promote programs for social causes.[46] They discovered that non-profit brands are more effective in their attempt to support the credibility of cause-related marketing programs than for-profit companies. However, they point out that effective branding for nonprofits is a complex task. Branding in the nonprofit sector must meet the needs of donors, as well to influence the public, governmental, and commercial partners. Voeth and Herbst also believe that a strong emotional attach-ment of donors to nonprofit organizations is a crucial part of nonprofit branding.[47] The authors examined brand personalities in the nonprofit sector to create a more system-atic framework of branding for the area of business. They believe that a strong emo-tional attachment of donors to nonprofit organizations is a crucial part of nonprofit branding. In spite of the fact that nonprofit organizations offer intangible benefits as opposed to a tangible product offered by commercial enterprises, the opportunity still exists for them to benefit from brand strategies. The fact of the matter is that the emo-tional attachment between donors (or customers for that matter) is at the forefront of all successful branding strategies. But for nonprofits in particular, the nature of the transaction between organization and donor is driven by a social as opposed to an economic motive.[48]

BRAND AWARENESS

Baghi and Gabrielli explored the role of awareness for for-profit versus nonprofit brands in co-branding. As the result of the quantitative study the authors discovered that in the collaboration between a commercial and a nonprofit brand, brand awareness doesn't change consumer feeling about a branded cause.[49] Therefore, following the cause that is meaningful is more important than finding the public that feels passionate about the brands themselves. They point out that the marketing effort is not effective at changing the way a consumer perceives the relevance of a social issue, so one could conclude from this that branding alone cannot be used to influence the consumer's perception on the relevance of the issue, and hence, nonprofits should focus on those people whom they are relatively sure will already know or care about a particular social issue.

Furthermore, they discovered that consumers are generally skeptical and unbelieving about for-profit organizations that promote social cause programs. According to the authors, a social cause may not increase sales for poorly made products. However, strong branding that collaborates in a cause-related campaign will get the most benefits since the customer will be willing to pay extra for it. Furthermore, the research helped determine that people are willing to pay more for well-known brands.

COLLABORATIVE BRANDING STRATEGIES

Dickinson and Barker looked at the phenomenon of co-branding alliances between nonprofit and commercial companies.[50] According to the authors, nonprofit organizations frequently benefit from alliances with commercial organization as it helps them build strong brand equity. Brand images of nonprofit and for-profit organizations can merge in actual products (e.g., a bundle offer), or symbolically (e.g., in advertising). The authors argue that it is imperative that the right partner be used by the nonprofit organization. Since brand alliances use the power of transferred brand feelings and meaning, the right fit between brands is very important. Based on their research results, they discovered that the perceived fit is achieved by two factors: High ratings of original brand attitudes and a familiarity with brands. Moreover, the authors discovered that the more favorable the initial attitudes are about the brands, the more positively the alliance is evaluated.

Randle, Leisch, and Dolnicar examined how volunteering organizations use competitive and collaborative strategies to attract volunteers.[51] As the authors explained, traditionally, charity organizations operated to contribute to the public good without focusing heavily on competition. Nowadays, however, nonprofit organizations face a lot of competition for limited resources (volunteers, donations, etc.), and need to use competitive strategies to achieve their goals. The authors studied the volunteer market in Australia to learn whether nonprofit organizations can effectively implement collaborative strategies instead of competitive strategies. As the result of the research of the permission based online panel, the authors measured image perceptions of volunteering organizations, considerations of the organizations, motivations for volunteering, and social-demographic characteristics of potential volunteers. As the result of their research, the authors determined that potential volunteers differ in their motivations, and should therefore be targeted based on their knowledge.

In addition to published theoretical and empirical research, executives in nonprofit organizations largely align with these key findings. According to Emily Callahan, CMO of St. Jude's fundraising organization, more spending in advertising may prevent nonprofit organizations from investing more in the programs that really help people. Cause-related campaigns are something that people are inclined to talk about. Successful nonprofit executives believe that nonprofit marketers should leverage social media, WOM, and online videos to spread their message virally. Moreover, as stated by Jeff Davidoff, CMO of One, a nonprofit organization focused on combating extreme poverty and preventable illnesses in impoverished parts of the world, collaboration with other companies and celebrities is most effective when the partners represent the right fit. The recommendations of the nonprofit CMOs in the article correlate with the previous recommendations made by researchers, which further demonstrates the relevance of the research knowledge in practical nonprofit branding.

BRANDING OF POLITICAL ORGANIZATIONS

Whereas the branding of politicians was covered under a separate chapter on the branding of services and people, the inclusion of political organizations in this chapter sets forth some unique circumstances and issues that must be taken into consideration when one looks at a political party from an organizational view. If one were to look at the role of political parties in other parts of the world outside the U.S., they would find that in many countries, the branding in politics centers on the party, the political leader of the party. However, in the U.S., the branding in politics calls for a two-pronged approach, where the political party establishes its own brand over time, regardless of who is the titular leader of the party, and that is then impacted by the specific issues of a particular political campaign and the person who is nominated to be the presidential nominee chosen at a party convention. In light of this issue, and to further reinforce the notion that branding strategies become more challenging and complex as one moves from a tangible product to an organization, the unique characteristics of politics adds another layer of complexity on top of the conclusions drawn in the chapter thus far on corporate and nonprofit branding.

Choosing a political leader or a political organization is a serious step that has long-term implications. Popular political organizations can influence the electorate and make it form a set of mental images related to a specific political figure or a political party. Corporate brand images of political organizations and politicians are prone to be transformed and even misinterpreted by voters. Given the importance of the role of differentiating oneself in a political campaign from other candidates, it is critical that the role of political party branding be understood as it works hand in hand with the choice of candidates within a party to shape the image of the organization, which can prove to determine the success or failure of a political candidate.

Political parties definitely form brands, and they spend a lot of resources to sustain themselves as brands. According to Singer, a promised "benefit" that is clearly stated and trusted, can provide a lasting success to a political organization, hence the influence of the brief but clear themes the former presidential candidates heavily leveraged throughout their campaigns.[52] Reeves, de Chernatony, and Carrigan argue that branding in politics has become essential in capitalist societies, and political parties are becoming more marketing driven in spite of them being ideology-driven historically.[53] This is due to the fragmentation of traditional political parties into segments of the electorate that have unique issues and concerns, and the ability to uncover this type of information through the use of more advanced technological tools, including Social Media and Big Data to effectively communicate with citizens.[54] Branding of political organizations consists of many dimensions. Both the internal relations within the political organization and the external interactions with the voter shape the political brand. Phipps, Brace-Govan, and Jevons insist that the consumer's role in political branding is crucial. Unfortunately, many politicians often overlook the voter's role.[55] As the authors state, political parties historically have relied on product-oriented strategies. The authors argue that voters are able to recreate a brand and make its identity different from the sponsor's brand. This particular phenomenon can be seen manifesting in anti-movements. However, a modern approach toward political marketing and branding emphasizes the importance of "customer-oriented" political strategies, especially in democratic societies.[56]

Engaged voters seek real communication with political organizations. Phipps, Brace-Govan, and Jevons explain that communication with the public and local communities beyond elections can be defined as the permanent campaign, namely the use of political marketing methods for the use of running government.[57, 58] Moreover, the authors define the growth of "issue-driven activism" as a point of real contact between politicians and communities. The connection between a political party and their community when campaigning on key issues helps establish relationships that further supplement the politician's brand equity and credibility.

According to Phipps, Brace-Govan, and Jevons, the political product is very similar to service because it is "intangible, perishable, heterogeneous and inseparable from the provider."[59] Because of the similarity to a service, the researchers claim that the political brand equity consists of two main elements: Brand Awareness (controlled communication such as advertising) and Brand Meaning (word of mouth). Consumers attribute qualities of a political party to its candidate the same way as they rely on the reputation of a company while buying products or services. Political parties constitute a brand entity where the image of the political party may have a more profound influence on voters than an individual political candidate. On the other hand, a political leader may also influence the brand of his/her political party through his/her activities. By establishing brand awareness along with brand meaning, the politician establishes a network of supporters that increases visibility to their campaign and values. As this network grows, the political brand continues to gain exposure and support, further enhancing the equity and credibility of the political brand of a political organization.

The shift which has taken place in the U.S. from ideologically-driven politics toward voter-driven politics is frequently identified in the scientific world by different authors.[60] In the light of the changes, the real challenge that political organizations face is the need to effectively apply brand management strategies in their day-to-day activities. However, some experts argue that the commercial brand management approach is not appropriate for political organizations. For example, French and Smith emphasize that the use of commercial brand models in political marketing can bring negative results, such as "narrowing the political agenda, increasing confrontation, demanding conformity of behavior/message and even increasing political disengagement at the local level" (Scammell).[61,62] But Reeves et al. insist that the brand management approach in politics is good when it helps meet the needs of voters.[63] This argument has been put forward forcefully by Newman.[64]

O'Cass and Voola propose that the resource-based view of political branding helps predict success or failure of political marketing campaigns.[65] As the authors state, political and marketing activities are the forming factors in all types of societies, and modern political marketing has evolved into long-term strategic marketing. Thus, the role of strategic marketing is to maintain a competitive advantage, one of the fundamental concepts that exists in all product and service marketing strategies for companies in the political for-profit and nonprofit sectors.[66] Resources are important for prosperity and success of a political organization. However, resources alone do not provide a competitive advantage.[67] The authors believe that, by analogy with commercial marketing, only unique capabilities help companies effectively use the resources they have. The brand of political parties and political leaders can be considered those unique capabilities in the political marketing context.

POLITICAL BRANDING VS. CORPORATE BRANDING

According to Wilner, similarities between corporate and political branding are rapidly disappearing.[68] According to the author, the role of market share is one of the most significant differences between political and corporate marketing. In politics, even a small difference between the candidates' market shares might be crucial for the victory of one party over its opponents. Furthermore, there also exist differences in advertising. Political advertising is "driven by the opposition research and breaking news," whereas consumer companies normally avoid using too much of negative commercial messages. The point here is that in the political marketplace, unlike the commercial marketplace, research is carried out to dig up "dirt" on an opponent, whether it is a particular politician, or leaders of a political party in an effort to discredit them in upcoming elections. In political marketing, the goal of campaign advertising is mainly to "destroy" the competition.[69]

According to Nightingale, political candidates are similar to major corporate brands in that they conduct the same extensive research, seek to differentiate themselves from the competition, create their value propositions and spend a lot of resources on building relationships with their target audiences.[70] Another important difference between political and corporate brands is that in corporate marketing number two brands might have a lot of loyalty and control a substantial market share, whereas a losing political candidate is quickly forgotten.[71] Just look at the results of any recent U.S. Presidential Election and it is obvious that the media loses interest in following the loser of a recent campaign, unless they have the ability to run again, and this is corroborated by public opinion polls.

IMPORTANCE OF INFLUENCERS AND GRASSROOTS

Phipps, Brace-Govan, and Jevons argue that political organizations have two brand images that can function separately: first, a corporate brand image that a political organization strives to project, and second, a brand image that appears organically through direct interactions between political parties and their engaged voters.[72] According to their research conclusions, involved voters are able to communicate political brand images through word of mouth to influence other voters. Therefore, politicians and political parties should pay special attention to highly-involved grassroots groups of voters, as they are able to shape political brands. Furthermore, they argue that a positive brand image of a politician formed by a community can significantly improve negative brand image of a party. Moreover, the more politicians are engaged with the influence groups in the electorate, the stronger is the influence of the politicians' personal brand equities. Personal brand equities of politicians merge with corporate brand equities of their political parties to create unique brand images and strengthen customer loyalty.

One would have to conclude from the review of the literature in this area that the branding of political organizations is based on the same strategies and theoretical frameworks that are applied in commercial marketing. The modern political marketing movement is driving political organizations around the world from ideologically-based strategies to voter-oriented strategies. The political brand is created and modified by the interactions between the community and politicians within a democratic political system. Understanding of the voter is crucial, with the main goal of political organizations focused on how well their brand is defined and how effectively it meet the needs of their voters. As political marketing drives electoral votes, as opposed to traditionally ideology-driven votes, candidates must effectively employ the 3C model throughout their campaign. Careful consideration of channel, customer, and competition is equally as important in driving effective political organization brands as it is for developing effective corporate brands; however, the context and nuances of each of the 3Cs varies given the differences between these two types of entities.

CASE STUDIES OF CORPORATE AND NONPROFIT BRANDING

Case 1: LEGO

The re-branding strategy for the LEGO Corporation represents an example of a company that engaged in a successful corporate branding process as the result of the alignment of strategic vision, organizational culture, and stakeholder images.[73] Schultz and Hatch analyzed the history of the LEGO Company's corporate branding process, and identified the challenges that the company had been facing. Over the past several years, the toy industry has faced many changes, such as faster paced child development, growth of the digital world, rapid change of trends in the industry, as well as dependence on global mega-brands, such as Star Wars and Harry Potter. In the late 1990s, the Lego brand was lagging behind the modern trends and was considered not cool among kids. The company wanted to regain its popularity and image without losing the heritage of the brand that is so attractive to parents. Another challenge was posed by the fact that LEGO has multiple brand extensions into software, lifestyle products, and accessories, which made the brand highly fragmented. The authors laid out the marketing challenges facing the company:

- ▶ Brand Positioning toward consumers ("dusty" image)
- ▶ Brand Positioning toward competitors (a need to regain territory in learning and development)
- ▶ Brand Architecture (multiple sub brands without connections)
- ▶ Brand Management (poorly aligned organizational processes and marketing channels)
- ▶ Communication (fragmented communication lacked common brand message)

To preserve the brand heritage and recreate a cohesive brand, LEGO top managers made a decision to reintegrate the company and to successfully reestablish the brand vision. They emphasized the importance of balancing conflicting elements at all stages of corporate rebranding during the creation of unique brand models. In their case study, they described the strategy that LEGO used to develop its global brand. The authors claimed that rebranding of a global company is an ongoing initiative that requires changes in the overall corporate strategy.

On the basis of their case study of LEGO, Schultz and Hatch created the Vision-Culture-Image model (VCI) that defines a successful corporate branding process as the alignment of strategic vision, organizational culture, and stakeholder images. According to the authors, "The LEGO Company enjoyed continuous growth and, as measured in 2001 by Young and Rubicam's Brand Asset Evaluator, the brand was ranked the seventh most respected among families with children, following Coca-Cola, Kellogg, Disney, Levi's, Fisher-Price, and Pampers."[74]

Case 2: McDonald's

Whiteside explored the way McDonald's has been addressing its critics, and how the company has supported its loyal followers.[75] McDonald's is a company that traditionally gets a lot of criticism. Consumers hold negative perceptions about the brand for their perceived role of obesity, low food quality standards (using "pink slime" in hamburgers), and poor treatment of workers as the minimum wage debate gains traction. According to Whiteside, McDonald's actively monitors the conversations through social media to get a better understanding of the changing consumer sentiment and acts where a response is necessary. They have monitored the role of family bloggers, in particular on Twitter and Facebook, and more recently began to follow blogs on Pinterest. As part of this effort, McDonald's has been very actively addressing its critics in social media. The insights McDonald's has gathered prompted the company to take a series of steps to improve these negative perceptions. Now the company uses its brand ambassadors as communities that focus on some of their top-selling products, like the Big Mac and McRib, uses in-depth consumer research to better understand its new customers, and uses a human voice in their attempt to promote an image centered on fun and friendship. As a result of enhanced understanding and effective use of candid consumer feedback, McDonald's has shifted its negative brand perceptions and built up brand equity. The company still faces critics, as all brands do, but is no longer widely criticized for these key concerns to the same extent as they were prior to taking these steps to improve their brand image.

Case 3: APHA

APHA is an association of public health professionals who advocate for selected citizens. It is an organization that has attempted to integrate a large body of work to document how federal policy has influenced its members. Their mission includes five different goals:[76, 77, 78]

1. To provide a center for those people who are committed to population health, in an effort to help solve issues for their members.

2. To identify the best practices based on their research.

3. To enrich the lives of all citizens.

4. To work to prevent disease and injury and to enable those who are faced with any disaster to be able to respond to it.

5. To increase the quality of life for all members from a health perspective.

The role of branding in this organization is complicated by the very wide range of issues that APHA supports. For every decision they make on branding, there needs to be a consistent effort to keep in mind how it is communicated vis-à-vis their logo, fonts, and language. They believe that a consistent brand increases the likelihood that they will receive a positive response from anyone who is trying to establish whether or not they are carrying out the goals of their organization. In this effort to create a consistent brand identity in their marketplace, they hired Metropolitan Group to assess and make recommendations for changes to their corporate brand identity. This objective was carried out by bringing together the opinions of those people who work closely with the organization, as well as the opinions of other public health professionals. The net result of this arrangement was the development of a new tagline and logo. Despite the various objectives and activities of the organization, an effective use of one clear, consistent message delivered through standardized logos, colors, and messaging helped clarify and consolidate the disparate parts of the organization into a single, unified brand. This re-branding effort gave the APHA a new sense of commitment as they sought to achieve their goals and mission as a nonprofit organization.

STRATEGIC BRAND FOCUS

The conclusions drawn from the literature review in corporate and nonprofit branding suggests that the role of competition is expanded to include multiple stakeholders who may become a factor in the successful branding strategies among corporations. Due to the very public nature of corporations, as well as nonprofit organizations, and their rather high profile in multiple sectors in society, it becomes more important to understand how branding is affected across these stakeholders.

The customer in corporate branding is very much influenced by the different channels that can be used by organizations selling various products and services, making it difficult for these kinds of companies to maintain a consistent image in the mind of the various stakeholders involved. This is magnified in the nonprofit world where organizations seek the support of many different stakeholders, oftentimes through different channels. For example, an organization that seeks to support immigrants who recently enter the U.S. may have great difficulty in reaching out to these people with the aid of workers in government organizations that are on the front line to support them after they enter the country. As laws change in a country, the channels used to work with these people could also change, where support groups and other nongovernment agencies become more or less important depending on the legal status of these people.

For example, as immigration in the United States becomes increasingly restricted, immigrants are exposed to a new set of risks, challenges, and fears when immigrating to this country. As a result, feelings of fear or discrimination often prevent immigrants from trusting American entities, including nonprofits designed to support them. Therefore, channel strategy is an important factor for nonprofits to consider in order to reach immigrants and foster a sense of trust and security. Many nonprofits that work with immigrants focus on creating a community and leverage that base as a channel for communication. Because the community includes both nonprofit workers as well as other immigrants, new immigrants find it easier to acclimate to their new home when surrounded by others going through similar situations. The community itself can be comprised of various sub-channels, like events, social media pages, 24-hour telephone hotline access, e-mail, etc., in order to foster a constant sense of connectedness. The greater the connectivity of the community, the more the community feels at ease to trust one another, build relationships, and ultimately find value in the nonprofits' activities and services. In the case of nonprofits focusing on immigration, the need to exude feelings of security and belongingness drive the channel selection, and are critical components of the success of the programs and ability to fulfill their mission of helping immigrants.

CONCLUSION

Three general categories of organizations are discussed in this chapter: corporations, nonprofits, and political organizations. Each type of organization has a similar set of general guidelines to establish brand identities, but given their differences in goals, operations, and composition, specific best practices are refined depending on the type of organization.

Corporations

For profit corporations have a heightened burden to strengthen the reputation of the company as a whole in the eyes of key stakeholders. Although investors are typically the top prioritized group of stakeholders for corporations, internal employees, consumers, and the media are also critical audiences to consider. Competition for corporations is a driving force in brand strategy, as corporations thrive or fail depending on their ability to effectively navigate a competitive environment, and creating an effective brand to showcase differentiation is therefore instrumental to the success of the brand and the company as a whole. Communicating a consistent message to these various stakeholders that effectively captures the brand, values, and identity that differentiates the company from competitors is challenging and complex. This is why management support and clarity is vital. The corporate brand must start at the top, have full support, and be communicated uniformly down through the various levels of employees. As a result, the consistent internal message translates to a consistent external message received by the various stakeholders. Management can consider using traditional branding frameworks, like the 4Ps, to develop the brand strategy, but the consistent communication of it to the various stakeholders is ultimately critical to the success of the brand and overall company.

Nonprofit Organizations

Nonprofits are similar to corporations in the sense that they also have a responsibility to their stakeholders, but the nature of their responsibility varies from that of a for-profit company. Because nonprofits have primary objective to maximize social welfare as opposed to maximize profit as corporations aim to do, different expectations apply to nonprofit brands. Donors are key stakeholders for nonprofits, along with employees, the media, and the general public, and hence a need to create an effective brand image to attract donors is vital to the business continuity of a nonprofit organization. Additionally, emotional branding is more important to develop for nonprofits than other entities given the nature of the objective to enhance social welfare. To appeal to donors, nonprofits must consider how to leverage emotional branding effectively to communicate their message clearly in a way that will resonate with this critical group of stakeholders. Clarity of the brand identity as well as ease of access to information are two important aspects of the brand. Donors must be able to understand the mission of the nonprofit, as well as how their money will be used, to persuade them to invest in the cause of the organization. For nonprofits, competition is much less of a focus, once again given the difference in primary objective from corporations. Therefore, the use of collaboration is beneficial for nonprofits because it reduces marketing spending (relieving budgetary constraint challenges nonprofits generally face) as well as helps increase brand exposure and awareness through building relationships with outside entities. Nonprofits can partner with corporations, other nonprofits, community leaders and influencers, media sources, or political organizations to leverage certain capabilities and further enhance their brand identity without the risk of competition eroding brand value as it would for corporations. Given the differences in the structure, goals, and processes of nonprofits, it is important to note the development of this brand strategy varies from that of a political organization or a corporation.

Political Organizations

Organizational branding for political entities also carries some similarities to corporate branding, though it includes some unique differences that must be addressed in the brand strategy development phase. Similar to corporate brands, competition is a key factor to consider and mitigate against for political organizational branding. Hence, the use of negative advertisements is a common strategy employed by politicians to combat competitors while attempting to boost their own political brand credibility. Furthermore, the importance of relationship building for political brands necessitates forming community connections through social issue activism, which is an important part of political organization branding that is not necessarily as important for corporate branding. Grassroots campaigns and social influencers are also uniquely critical to political organizational branding. As part of creating a competitive advantage, politicians must effectively foster trust among community constituents to earn their vote, which requires them to identify the key causes and issues they care most about, and develop a persuasive stance as to why they are the best candidate to effectively address those concerns if elected. Segmenting potential voters on these issues, as well as identifying high and low involvement voters, helps politicians tailor their message to be most effective in various communities. Because of the lasting effects of political branding, the values of brand must be maintained long-term to keep voters engaged and loyal to a certain party or set of candidates (typically Republican or Democrat). The need to address competition effectively, understand the voting audience, and communicate through appropriate channels are key considerations for a political brand. As political marketing drives electoral votes, as opposed to traditionally ideology-driven votes, political organizations must craft a campaign that encompasses relationship marketing, competitive differentiation, and effective segmentation. Once again, we see that the distinct characteristics of political organizations vary from those of a corporation or nonprofit, and are critical components to consider in political brand strategy development.

Endnotes

1. Balmer and Greyser, Corporate marketing: Integrating corporate identity, corporate branding, corporate communications, corporate image and corporate reputation, 2006.
2. Roll, 2004.
3. Balmer and Greyser, Corporate marketing: Integrating corporate identity, corporate branding, corporate communications, corporate image and corporate reputation, 2006.
4. Hatch and Schultz, Bringing the corporation into corporate branding, 2003.
5. Aaker, 1996.
6. Hatch and Schultz, Bringing the corporation into corporate branding, 2003.
7. Einwiller and Will, 2002.
8. Roll, 2004.
9. Balmer and Greyser, Corporate marketing: Integrating corporate identity, corporate branding, corporate communications, corporate image and corporate reputation, 2006.
10. Balmer and Greyser, Corporate marketing: Integrating corporate identity, corporate branding, corporate communications, corporate image and corporate reputation, 2006.
11. Hatch and Schultz, Bringing the corporation into corporate branding, 2003.
12. Einwiller and Will, 2002.
13. Hatch and Schultz, Toward a theory of brand co-creation with implications for brand governance, 2010.
14. Hogl and Hupp, 2005.
15. Roll, 2004.
16. Laforet and Saunders, 2005.
17. Einwiller and Will, 2002.
18. Hatch and Schultz, Bringing the corporation into corporate branding, 2003.
19. Balmer, Corporate identity, corporate branding and corporate marketing-seeing through the fog, 2001.
20. Urde, 2003.
21. de Chernatony, 1999.
22. Asmus, 2009.
23. Harris and de Chernatony, 2001.
24. Aaker, 1996.
25. Einwiller and Will, 2002.
26. Hatch and Schultz, Bringing the corporation into corporate branding, 2003.
27. Hatch and Schultz, Toward a theory of brand co-creation with implications for brand governance, 2010.
28. Fan, 2005.
29. Fan, 2005.
30. Fan, 2005.

31. Fan, 2005.
32. de Bussy, Ewing, Berthon, and Pitt, 2002.
33. de Bussy, et al., 2002.
34. Laforet and Saunders, 2005.
35. Laforet and Saunders, 2005.
36. Laforet and Saunders, 2005.
37. Aaker, 1996.
38. Hatch and Schultz, Bringing the corporation into corporate branding, 2003.
39. Einwiller and Will, 2002.
40. Hogl and Hupp, 2005.
41. Urde, 2003.
42. Balmer, Corporate identity, corporate branding and corporate marketing-seeing through the fog, 2001.
43. Einwiller and Will, 2002.
44. Stride and Lee, 2007.
45. Stride and Lee, 2007.
46. Baghi and Gabrielli, 2012.
47. Voeth and Herbst, 2008.
48. Voeth and Herbst, 2008.
49. Baghi and Gabrielli, 2012.
50. Dickinson and Barker, 2007.
51. Randle, Leisch and Dolnicar, 2013.
52. Singer, 2002.
53. Reeves, de Chernatony, and Carrigan, Building a political brand: Ideology or voter-driven strategy, 2006.
54. B. I. Newman, The Marketing Revolution in Politics: What Recent U.S. Presidential Campaigns Can Teach Us About Effective Marketing, 2016.
55. Phipps, Brace-Govan and Jevons, 2010.
56. B. I. Newman, The Marketing Revolution in Politics: What Recent U.S. Presidential Campaigns Can Teach Us About Effective Marketing, 2016.
57. Phipps et al., 2010.
58. B. I. Newman, The Handbook of Political Marketing, 1999.
59. Phipps et al., 2010.
60. B. I. Newman, Reinforcing Lessons for Business from the Marketing Revolution in U.S. Presidential Politics: A Strategic Triad, 2016.
61. French and Smith, 2010.
62. Scammell, 1999.
63. Reeves et al., 2006.
64. B. I. Newman, The Marketing of the President, 1994.
65. O'Cass and Voola, 2011.
66. B. I. Newman, The Marketing Revolution in Politics: What Recent U.S. Presidential Campaigns Can Teach Us About Effective Marketing, 2016.
67. O'Cass and Voola, 2011.
68. Wilner, 2012.

69. Wilner, 2012.
70. Nightingale, 2012.
71. Nightingale, 2012.
72. Phipps et al., 2010.
73. Schultz and Hatch, The cycles of corporate branding: the case of the Lego company, 2003.
74. Schultz and Hatch, The cycles of corporate branding: the case of the Lego company, 2003.
75. Whiteside, 2013.
76. Wright, 2015.
77. Matthews, 2015.
78. Tumulty, Rucker and Costa, 2015.

CHAPTER 6

BRANDING OF NATIONS

INTRODUCTION

The branding of nations involves many of the same tactics and considerations that have been put forward for products, services, people, and organizations. However, since this level of branding includes a wide variety of people and organizations, as well as the potential for a different assortment of products and services sold within a country, the likelihood of using the same branding strategy for multiple countries becomes less likely. This is because every country has a unique culture and makeup that may call for attention to certain considerations that one would not make for another country.

For example, the branding of the U.S. as compared to China involves very different issues given that each country operates on the basis of a different political system. In light of this, and the different historical makeup of each, branding strategies will reflect unique characteristics of each country. Furthermore, due to the unique makeup of each of the political systems in the two countries, the channels that are used to carry out a branding strategy will be quite different. Unlike the U.S., where the media operates as an independent institution, China is in a position to rely on the government-run media to reinforce existing beliefs and attitudes to brand the country in the minds of their citizens. However, the branding of China to the outside world can rely on the use of the same channels that are used in the U.S. During the Olympics in 2008, there were news organizations from all over the world that reported back to their respective countries, including news organizations from the U.S., all of them relying on similar channels to report on the events that took place, using both traditional and

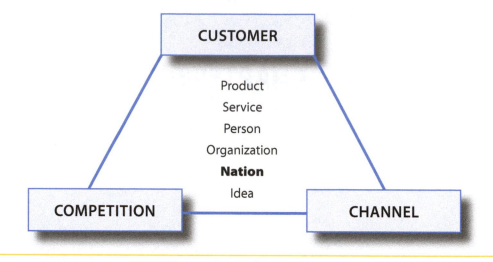

social media outlets. It is important to note that during this period of time, China did restrict the use of certain social media outlets on computers that were accessed within the country.

Nation branding brings together much of the literature and best practices reported in the previous chapters, all of which when aggregated across the different entities covered, represent an overall impression of a nation through the products and services they sell, as well as through the individuals and organizations who represent different sectors of society that may be unique to one country, but not another. For example, in some countries, there may be a predominance of products sold that are different and unique to that country. Cuba is known for their production of cigars, while Austria is known for its production of sweets. In Austria, it is commonplace for people to go to coffeehouses during the day to get their favorite sweets, along with a cup of coffee known as one of the best in the world. But in a country like Japan, people are more likely to be visiting sushi restaurants in the afternoon, and having a cup of tea with their food.

This discussion can be extended to other countries, along different product lines, like the manufacturing of automobiles, defensive weapons, and robotics, depending on the level of economic performance of the country. All nations represent brands at each of the different entity levels discussed in previous chapters, which when taken together, present a picture of a nation to anyone trying to understand how a country is defined in peoples' minds. Our discussion in this chapter goes beyond this level of analysis to include considerations that have been reported in the literature along some key areas that will be useful in distinguishing and separating one nation's brand from another, including: effective techniques for the creation of brand equity of nations, countries and places; the phenomenon of nation branding as a commercial practice; the examination of modern states of nation branding and the differences between that and commercial branding; a comprehensive overview of nation branding, the nation brand in particular parts of the world, and the differences between nation branding and product-country image.[1, 2, 3, 4, 5, 6]

DEFINITION OF A NATION VS. NATIONAL BRAND

The branding of nations is a relatively new concept. At present, a number of scholars have explored the topic. One of the more comprehensive works devoted to this subject was carried out by Fan (2010, p. 98), who defined a nation brand as, "the total sum of all perceptions of a nation in the minds of international stakeholders, which may contain some of the following elements: people, place, culture, language, history, food, fashion, famous faces (celebrities), global brands and so on."[7] He believes that nation branding is a multi-dimensional term that can be divided into the following subcategories: country branding, destination branding, public diplomacy, and national identity. Fan also made the point that national brand is not the same as nation brand. National brand is a signature product of a certain nation, whereas nation brand, as discussed above, is a master-brand that includes various sub-categories. He emphasized that a nation's brand identity is defined as its self-perception, whereas a nation's brand image is an outside perception toward the country itself. Moreover, reputation is an external perception that can be defined as an external feedback mechanism on the credibility of the nation. In an effort to improve national reputation, which is often the main goal of nation branding, he recommends that positive qualities of the nation be communicated.

Anholt developed a Nation Brand Index (NBI) to analyze the global opinion about America's brand.[8] The index is an assessment tool that includes the following six criteria: tourism, people, culture and heritage, investment and immigration, foreign and domestic policy, and export brands. He argued that to strengthen its nation brand, a country needs to "live" it, which means that all of the nation's constituents (government, businesses, people, public diplomacy, etc.) not only need to create communications about the nation that are attractive in nature, but stressed the importance of a nation needing to live up to its mission and vision.

Nation branding is also impacted by the perceptions of a country on the basis of its international policy. For example, Garbacz-Rawson analyzed how the U.S. international policy helped shape the perceptions of the country, and discovered that the concept of the political national brand lies within the nation brand of a country.[9] The two concepts are interrelated, with the nation brand being created by the political foundation of the country, which is based on the actions and policies of the nation as well as those of the political figures. In an effort to support this hypothesis, the author used Anholt's nation-branding hexagon identified in the previous paragraph.[10] The author insists that the center of the model is a government-centered strategy, which puts the burden of the brand development strategy for the country on the back of the government. Furthermore, public diplomacy, which is referred to as soft power, directly correlates with the nation brand.

According to the definition of soft power put forward by Joseph Nye Jr., a country's political image serves as a way to create positive perceptions internationally.[11] So, through national political branding, a competitive identity for a country is created. Political leaders are ultimately the most visible representatives of the national political brand, and through their words and actions, a nation's brand is developed. However, according to this thinking, the role of foreign policy carries even more significance and potential to shape the perceptions of nations.[12]

THE INTEGRATED MARKETING COMMUNICATION (IMC) APPROACH

Integrated Marketing Communication (IMC) is a holistic approach toward the strategic management of brands.[13] The branding of nations can effectively be achieved by the IMC approach. However, it is often a very challenging task due to the fact that there are a big number of stakeholders that struggle to coordinate their activities. Dinnie, Melewar, Seidenfuss, and Musa present several important implications for the branding of nations: First, they stress the importance of the coordination of inter-organizational entities, which include not only a nation's key public sector organizations, but also those organizations and other private organizations that play a role in the successful implementation of a country's nation branding goals.[14] Secondly, organizations need to collaborate with other countries in an effort to solidify the relationships with them. Third, the level of coordination between collaborating countries needs to be outlined. And finally, policymakers need to determine the correct balance of their global approach to nation branding activities.

The use of an Integrated Marketing Communication approach put forward by Dinnie et al. also proposes that national branding is accomplished by the integrated work of multiple state organizations.[15] The authors examined how various state organizations, such as export promotion organizations (EPOs), investment agencies (IAs), national tourism organizations (NTOs), and embassies, use an integrated marketing communications (IMC) approach. The research centers on the Association of Southeast Asian Nations (ASEAN) region, which has a population of more than 450 million people, representing a very lucrative market that needs to develop a brand identity that goes beyond a single nation, and includes multiple nations. The logic of branding a nation applies as well to a region of nations, such as the ASEAN region, just as it would to the European Union (EU), or any other block of countries that seeks to identify itself with a brand identity. The complexity of branding a region of nations is a more complicated process, as it must take into account the similarities and differences between the nations in the region in an effort at identifying a universal identity that covers them all. The Brexit vote in the United Kingdom that resulted in a majority of voters supporting the exit of the UK from the European Union represents the difficulty of ensuring that a regional brand identity across countries reflects a consensus between nations on key issues. The branding of regions, even though it may be more complicated to achieve, indicates that there must be some common themes across which nations agree in the same way that there needs to be a consensus within a nation across themes that citizens agree with for a brand strategy.

The use of marketing and consumer research to extract the correct themes for a nation is one of the most important tasks that must be carried out when a nation seeks to define its brand identity. The research must be carried out across a wide range of subjects that reflects the nation's population as a whole. It also needs to account for the perception of the nation from a macro-analysis perspective, looking at the opinion of the majority of the citizens with respect to the economy, culture, political makeup, etc., all of which taken together constitute an overall brand identity. One could argue that leaders of nations seek to brand their country in the minds of its citizens with a focus on those issues that the leader is interested in reinforcing in an effort to keep his or her position intact. For example, the case of Vladimir Putin in Russia represents a leader who has sought to re-brand his country after the fall of the USSR, and the dismantling of that regional power, in the minds of his citizens as a military power in the world. This has been impacted by the economic circumstances of Russia which are tied to the price of oil, a commodity that fluctuates due to the role of other world economies that produce it. Without the benefit of a strong economy, it makes Mr. Putin's efforts to re-brand Russia as a world power that much more complicated. One can only assume that even Mr. Putin is relying on research to aid in his branding efforts.

Most countries rely heavily on the public perception of citizens' assessment of their nation with respect to tourism, investment, and other cultural indicators to determine how best to promote their nation brand. Kim, Shim, and Dinnie examined nine countries (Egypt, Italy, Korea, Japan, United States, Singapore, Sweden, China, and Brazil) and their relationships with the public perceptions of tourism, country of origin, residence, and investment.[16] A total of 1,221 responses were obtained, and the authors determined that the main facets of a nation brand are defined along the lines of leadership, excitement, sophistication, tradition, and peacefulness. According to the results of their study, the authors found that the different brand personality dimensions produce different intentions in the public (e.g., tourism, attractiveness for investors, or immigration factors), thus offering valuable insights into the branding of nations.

THE ROLE OF MEGA-EVENTS

Mega-events, such as the Olympic Games, can be used by countries to reinforce and/ or alter their nation brand identity. Heslop, Nadeau, O'Reilly, and Armenakyan examined the connection between brand images of mega-events (e.g., Olympic Games) and brand images of countries that host the events.[17] According to their research, image transfers and impacts on brand images for mega-events and host countries that are interconnected in the minds of tourists, sponsors, and the general public. Sporting mega-events such as the Olympic Games can offer the host nation a legitimate way to present and promote their national identities on a global scale. In their study, the authors examined two host countries for Olympic Games: Canada and China. Based on the results of the study, the authors emphasized that partner selection and co-branding alliances between countries and mega-events should be carefully managed, as the reputational effects can affect the participating parties.

The connection between a nation and a mega-event should create a meaningful emotional entity among all of the stakeholders. If a country that violates freedom and human rights of its citizens hosts a mega-event that promotes freedom, it creates a cognitive dissonance and negative attitudes in the public and the involved stakeholders. Through the transference of meaning, the brand image of the event can be tarnished. At the same time, the reputation of a hosting country can be affected by the mega-events that it hosts.[18] In an effort to get a better understanding of the tactics behind nation branding, we turn to a detailed analysis of how this process has played out recently in selected countries around the world.

CASE STUDIES OF NATION BRANDING

Case #1: China

One of the more significant nation branding campaigns in history that has relied on all of the modern tools of marketing is the case of China under President Xi Jinping. Soon after President Donald Trump entered the White House on a campaign built on a strong nationalist and populist theme, President Jinping sought to re-position the brand identity of his nation. Prior to Donald Trump's presidential victory in the 2016 election, China had been in the process of a multi-year re-branding campaign that was built on a very basic theme, not unique to China, referred to as the "Chinese Dream." The term began in earnest in 2013, with the new regime of President Xi Jinping, who sought to redefine the ideals of his country in the minds of the Chinese people around the theme of a more powerful China on the world stage that needed to be recognized internally before others would even think of recognizing them on a global stage. China sought to be recognized as both an economic and military power. One could even argue that this dream concept came into being with the 2008 Beijing Olympic Games, hosted by China, that thrust their culture onto the world stage.

Soon after Donald Trump pulled out of the Trans-Pacific Partnership (TPP), President Jinping wasted very little time to take the opportunity to present his country as the new global business leader, a statement of purpose that came to light at the 2017 Davos, where he gave a speech to this effect. The re-branding strategy was built around the protectionist positioning of the U.S. under President Trump, who decided that it was time to pull back from a policy put into place by his predecessor, President Obama, who argued that it was necessary to form as many global partners as possible to succeed in the future. The re-branding of China is now centered on the notion of Xi's country as a new global leader, namely a country over the past thirty years that has been transformed economically into a serious player on the global stage. One could ask the rhetorical question: How likely is it that China will be successful in this new branding opportunity, especially in light of the fact that the country has been under communist rule since the founding of the People's Republic of China in 1949 by Chairman Ma Zedong?

The answer to this question lies in the power of branding, and the ability of even a nation to enlist all of the best practices one would find in the branding of other entities that come the closest to nation branding, namely people and organizations. By definition, all countries have leaders, people, who enlist the help and support from many other people within a country to drive the policy of the country, regardless of political orientation, be it a democracy, market economy, socialist, or communist driven country. Organizations are also driven by CEO's, who with the help of people under that person in key positions of power, lead the organization, regardless of whether it is a for-profit or nonprofit driven company. So, the case of a nation is multiple steps more complex than the running of an organization, subject to the public opinion of people within the country, as well as the public opinion of the world. This leads us now to the state of affairs in China, representing a brand, unique to all other brands on the world stage, but very interesting to study from the perspective of a nation in the midst of a strategic pivot.

The speech given by President Jinping at Davos in 2017 was the introduction of the nation to the world as the country whose dream is moving forward, one could argue, in a similar vein as the United States did under President Bill Clinton who won election in 1992 and re-election in 1996 on the back of a campaign strategy built around the American Dream.[19] In his speech, Jinping offered to make his country open to other countries to do business with, and at the same time, taking a political swipe at Donald Trump by speaking out against a protectionist stand for nations in a time of global expansion. The branding strategy in place with this new move by China is not that different than the re-positioning of a company that seeks to take advantage of a "niche" held by a competitor when they identify an opportunity to compete more effectively for the same market.

China, under the leader of Xi, represents a classic case of the speed at which a nation can change the outward image of itself, but must then be watched closely to see whether or not policies are followed up in a consistent manner. This is the complexity of nation branding that separates it from the other brand categories covered in previous chapters, where an immediate brand makeover can work temporarily, but in the case of a nation, must be observed carefully over time to get an accurate measure of the impact of the makeover. Unlike the measures of brand popularity introduced earlier in the book, where sales alone can be an accurate measure of brand success, in the case of a nation, perhaps not different from the branding of a politician, public opinion becomes the ultimate test of success.

For the rest of the world that is watching China closely after its re-branding campaign, the real measure of success will come with the connection between the reality and perception that exists in China. For all of the grand statements made by Xi, the rest of the world will watch closely as the country is evaluated on different dimensions of openness that will either tie into the message of a new, open-minded, globally-directed China, or continue to be compared to the China of Mao Zedong, who put the country on a path of authoritarian rule for over sixty years that has kept public display of outbursts against the ruling government at a minimum, and the constant threat by the government against anyone who dares to challenge the leadership of Xi in any significant manner very real. But this is the complex nature of branding at a nation level.

Case #2: United States

At his inaugural speech in January 2017, President Donald Trump promised the world a different America, one where the world was introduced to a country that would put its own interests first before it reaches out to other countries around the world. This was the promise made by Donald Trump on the campaign trail, and one that was followed up in his inaugural address of a nation full of carnage, in disarray, that he, single-handedly, with the aid of his cabinet and staff, would change. One could argue that this was the most major re-branding effort in the U.S. not seen since the end of World War II.

The new brand of the U.S. was more clearly defined in the first week of Mr. Trump's presidency as he moved very quickly to alter the support of climate change policy that was put into place by President Obama. Along with this change came other executive orders that tied into immigration, placing on hold the ability of citizens coming from Muslim countries to enter the U.S., even if they were issued a visa. The immigration rule changes resulted in a public outburst around the country, and one could argue, around the world, clearly leading to another alteration of the brand that is clearly in the midst of a sea-change with the new Trump administration.

The alteration of the brand of the U.S. is vividly different than the one in China, where the country is ruled by an iron fist of one person, Xi Jinping, whereas in the U.S., the wheels of change operate in the form of a democracy, where it takes legislative change to alter existing laws. This process is moved along in the U.S. through the step-by-step change that takes place through the give-and-take, as well as the struggle for the ideological high ground between the two major political parties. The Democrats and Republicans, who dominate the Congress, in both the House of Representatives and

Senate, have the ultimate power to work along with the president in a re-branding process. Without the muscle of law behind the rhetoric of a president, the real brand identity of the U.S. cannot be changed, which brings one to the discussion of how Mr. Trump embarked on his branding strategy for America.

By single-handedly building a new brand identity for the Republican Party, Donald Trump has engaged in the first step that needs to come with a re-branding of the nation. As was discussed in previous chapters, political parties represent one example of organizational branding that carries with it unique characteristics and constraints that must be considered if one were to engage in such a process. Under a Trump administration, the Republican Party is changing before the very eyes of the nation, and along with the eyes of the nation are the eyes of the rest of the world. In most new administrations, it normally takes months before the ideological posturing of a new president takes hold. Not with the party of Donald Trump, who in his first week dismantled much of what President Obama worked hard to put into place over eight years, from healthcare, to immigration, to climate change, just to mention a few key executive orders put into place during his first week in office. At the same time, he re-positioned his party as warm and friendly to unions by meeting with union leaders his first week in office.

The Republican Party is turning from the party of big business to the party of populism, and at the same time, pitting the Republican Party not only against the Democratic Party, but against the media. This is a very clever maneuver to re-brand the nation through the elimination of the traditional dichotomous breakdown of the U.S. into two major parties running the country. In effect, it brings to mind a very different, but equally effective strategy that Bill Clinton used when he was in the White House, when he positioned his presidency around his leadership in the free world as opposed to the leader of a political party, and in the process, re-branded the U.S.[20]

Case #3: Russia

From a branding perspective, Russia represents a nation that has been very successful at establishing a brand identity within its own country that is seen by the majority of its citizens as a nation that has become a player on the international stage as a result of the actions of its president, Vladimir Putin. This branding strategy has not been as successful with the image of Russia outside of the country's borders after the occupation of Crimea in the Ukraine, as countries around the world accused Russia, and Mr. Putin in particular, as having taken actions that were seen as very aggressive. The point is that one can only judge the effectiveness of a nation's brand on the basis of the ability of a leader of a country to use it to carry out policies both internally and externally without opposition from a wide spectrum of publics. As the literature review in this chapter revealed, the notion of a nation brand versus a national brand are two very distinct and different constructs. To some degree, the nation brand is the inclusion of the perception of Russia by all stakeholders, including those who live within and outside the country, whereas the national brand can be broken down into different sub-categories that reflect the economic, cultural, and political makeup of this country.

Further complicating this discussion of Russia is the uniqueness and mysterious nature of this nation, what Winston Churchill once referred to as a puzzle wrapped up in a secret inside a riddle. This turns out to be clear when contemplating U.S. organizations marketing in Russia. Results from the last CMO Survey demonstrate that Russia is the international market with the highest sales growth rate. Sales are reported to have grown an average of 57 percent for U.S. organizations that designate Russia as their biggest worldwide market. This compares with India at 38 percent, China at 26 percent, and Brazil with 19 percent development.[21]

One of the most recent developments in Russia centers on their foray into the world of Olympics, when they hosted it in Sochi in 2014. As reported in this chapter, hosting a mega-event, like the Olympics, provides the possibility for a nation, like Russia, to present itself to the world in a way that it could not otherwise do because of the channel that opens up the Olympics to the rest of the world. Perhaps this is the most important implication of a mega-event, and that is the establishment of a channel of communication that cannot be matched by any other. Both the people around the world who watched the event, as well as those who were fortunate enough to attend agreed that Sochi, which was transplanted from an obscure town in the mountains of Russia to a winter wonderland, was a huge success that helped Russia to establish both its nation and national brand.

One part of the branding campaign that resulted from the Olympics for Russia was the opportunity for firms from outside Russia that participated in the venue to use it as a platform from which to expand their business ties to Russia. In the effort to re-establish their brand image as a friendlier and less hostile country (in a post-Crimea occupation period), sending a message to the world that more non-Russian companies began to do business with Russia after the Olympics only strengthens their brand image. Official sponsorships, as well as utilizing the Olympics for independent marketing events that piggybacked onto individual events, and athletes helped to increase brand awareness among Russian clients. Certainly, one risk that is taken with any mega-event in a country is the possibility that the event does not play out in a positive manner. Although there was the opening ceremony glitch with the Olympic rings which did not all light up as they should have, it did not have a material impact on the success of the event, and sent a strong message to anyone doing business in Russia that whereas there may be many opportunities, one must always prepare for the unexpected when interacting with this country.

Not only do mega-events shape the brand of a nation, but so does the inclusion and acceptance of a country by well-respected global groups that are connected through economic and political ties. But along with entrance into these organizations come the consequences of membership. For example, one would have to argue that Russia's entrance into the World Trade Organization (WTO) in 2012 led to lower tariffs on imported goods, making worldwide brands more competitive with Russian products. In an effort to prepare for that particular outcome, namely the potential explosion of Western goods available in Russia, and to more effectively compete outside of Russia, President Vladimir Putin challenged businesses within Russia to develop their own strong brands. Along this line of analysis, in 2013, Russia placed eighteenth in Bloomberg's Global Innovation Index Top 50 after placing fourteenth in 2012.[22]

Outside Moscow, a government-sponsored research campus called the Innovation Center helped to further establish Russia's national brand by inviting well-respected technology companies to participate in activities. One such company was Yandex, a Russian search engine company that had at one time a 60 percent market share of the overall industry compared to global counterparts such as Google. Another company that participated, Vkontakte(VK), actually outperformed Facebook and Kaspersky's Labs as one of the strongest software brands in the world. Sberbank (banking) as of late made several acquisitions to gain a global presence. Russian Standard is another company that has turned into a fast-growing worldwide vodka brand by following standards established by the industry. YotaPhone is still another example of an innovative mobile phone maker that features a two-sided Android system that combines both a smartphone and an e-reader. In their effort to establish their brand identity, these and other Russian organizations are quickly becoming sophisticated marketers who are able to compete effectively both at home and abroad, and thereby helping to shape the Russian brand.[23]

THE STRATEGIC BRAND FOCUS

The case of nation branding reveals the challenge of having to incorporate each of the other levels of branding discussed thus far in the book, as it relies on the contributions to the literature in each of the other previous four chapters on products, services, people, and organizations. From the point of view of the strategic brand focus that a country needs to take into consideration when embarking on a nation branding strategy, it is prudent at this point to refer to the 3C's.

The customer, in the case of a nation, goes beyond the country itself in question, and extends to every other country around the world. This is because public opinion impacts on the perception of a nation's image, and is subject to the opinions of other world leaders, as well as to the aggregated thinking and feelings of people around the world who communicate vis-à-vis social media.

Just take the case of the murder of Kim Jung Nan, stepbrother to the current leader of North Korea, Kim Jung Un. The story that unfolded across the globe after he was attacked by two women in the airport in Malaysia riveted global public opinion as the episode went viral. It was revealed that two women (who were both indicted on charges of murdering him) approached Mr. Kim Jung Nan as he was about to enter a boarding area at the airport, and in a matter of seconds, put a cloth on his face with the lethal chemical VX on it, and in minutes, he was dead. As the story circulated around the world, the opinion of world leaders as well as people of all stripes in different countries, reinforced the image of this nation, North Korea, as a brutal dictatorship that would stop at nothing to ensure its leader was in a strong position of power. The leading theory behind the killing was for Kim Jung Un, leader of North Korea, to demonstrate to the world that if anyone attempted to overthrow him, either from within or outside his country, there would not be an alternative to put into office in his place, as the people of North Korea support the family dynasty that has ruled the country for many decades now. The point here is that the image of North Korea was indelibly impacted by this act, and the nation brand affected by the whole world.

In the case of an organization doing business globally, the same cannot be said, as the brand of the organization will be primarily impacted by those opinion leaders doing business in the country it operates in, as well as in those countries outside of its borders it also does business in. In essence, the challenge to controlling the image of a nation is much more complicated from the customer perspective, because as one moves from an organization to a nation, the customer morphs into citizens and leaders of countries all over the world.

Beyond the more diversified and complex environment that nations operate in with respect to the range of customers (the first C), the competition (the second C) also presents itself as another level of complexity that makes nation branding so challenging. The competition for a company with respect to a product or service being sold, even in a global marketplace, can be much more easily defined and accounted for than can the competition of a nation. Countries operate on a geo-political chessboard on a daily basis, creating a strategic environment that is much more unpredictable and open to the possibility of a crisis erupting at any moment. Yes, corporations and even nonprofits each have crises to deal with on occasion, just as PwC did at the Academy Awards, or as BP or Carnival Cruise did in recent mishaps with respect to the oil spill by BP, and the accident that took place in Italy as a Carnival Cruise ship slammed into the harbor because of the captain's mistakes. Each of these crises were subject to human error, as was the Academy Awards debacle, but in light of how this affected each of these respective corporation's competitors, it was much less damaging than crises that occur between nations.

Finally, as was pointed out before in this chapter, the channels (the third C) that nations operate in are far more encompassing than those operated in by any person or organization, regardless of what is being sold to the customer, be it a product or service for that matter. The channels that exist for a nation are far more numerous than for any organization or person. As a rule, the more important the person, the more likely information will be conveyed through multiple channels about him or her, especially if it is the leader of a nation. Moreover, media is more interested in the actions of leaders of nations than sports celebrities, Hollywood actors, or even high-profile CEO's because in the end, regardless of what is being branded, the whole world is always resting on thin ice when it comes to international relationships between nations when there is a state of alarm in the world concerning terrorism. Without peace in the world, the brands of any product, service, person, or organization become much less important to ordinary people, who ultimately seek a safe haven for their children. Hence, the branding of nations brings us to the most complex level of branding discussed thus far in the book.

CONCLUSION

Nation branding is a widely complex level of branding which encompasses a variety of people, organizations, and political groups by which a brand reputation is formed by both the citizens of the nation as well as external groups. A nation's brand is defined by the total sum of all perceptions of the nations along various elements (including but not limited to people, place, culture/language, history, food, fashion, global brands, celebrities, etc.). Whereas a nation brand is a holistic approach to capturing the complexities and nuances of the nation's cultures, national branding refers simply to the signature product of a nation. Although these two terms appear similar, this distinction is important to note. Given the vast differences in cultural norms, traditions, and views among countries, each nation's brand is unique and hence a strategy that works for one country may not necessarily work for a different country that has different views, values, and practices.

In comparing the US to China, for example, the differences of the economic and political systems, namely capitalism versus communism, the approach and execution of nation brand strategy is quite different between these two countries. Norms and values that work for the American public don't necessarily align with norms and values in Chinese culture, and vice versa. As a result, these two nations project very different brands. Other smaller cultural nuances play a role in nation branding as well, such as etiquette, cuisine, dining, and traditions which also influence the nation's brand to a degree.

Because a nation's brand is represented in part by external influences, the importance of employing an integrated marketing communication (IMC) approach is an effective method to gather insights and form nation brand strategies. Essentially, the IMC approach leverages collaboration through international organizations (such as governmental bodies, tourism organizations, embassies, etc.) to develop a theme for the nation. The input from these external sources can direct brand strategy by providing valuable insights as to how outsiders perceive the nation to develop an understanding of brand identity. Understanding the brand identity as it's perceived by other international groups provides opportunity to improve or change aspects of the brand in order to enhance external brand perception and reputation. Along with the external perspective, the perception of citizens of the country is equally important to consider, particularly along the lines of leadership, excitement, sophistication, tradition, and peacefulness. The combination of internal and external perceptions drives brand strategy through identifying areas of opportunity as to what aspects of the brand need to be improved or changed to reach the ideal state.

Because of the complexities previously discussed surrounding culture, values, etc., among different countries, nation branding is best exemplified through discussion of a few case studies to highlight how different countries approached nation branding differently. While the book discusses several countries in more detail, the general ideas can be summarized in comparing two key cases: China against the United States.

China built a brand around the "Chinese Dream," intending to communicate China's power to the rest of the world and establish a more powerful role on a global scale. This was further solidified in the 2008 Olympics hosted in Beijing, where China was spotlighted with the entire world observing the country and learning more about its culture from the media attention the games brought across the globe. However, after Donald Trump took office in 2017 and declared the United States' intent to establish global partners, China aimed to accelerate its brand from being internationally influential to an international leader. While it is too soon to draw conclusions as to whether this re-branding strategy will be successful or not, it is a visible shift in China's objective which will affect the world from a political and economic perspective to some extent. Similarly, the United States is in the process of re-branding the nation following the election of Donald Trump, who has very different and strong views toward America's brand than his predecessors. Trump's "America first" stance has affected political ties internationally as well, through reduced funding for various international groups and organizations as well as Trump's vocal intention to continuously prioritize America's benefit over that of any other country, affecting trade deals and potentially creating penalties and fines for global business activity. Moreover, Trump's idealized brand focuses heavily on boosting militarization to further solidify the United States as a global superpower, and his intent to invest heavily in the United States armed forces to combat terror threats against the country are key aspects of this re-brand objective. Once again, the effects of this re-brand strategy are yet to be understood, as it takes quite a bit of time to understand the implications and success of branding a nation. However, it is evident that Trump's actions to develop this brand have influenced international perception of America as a country, from a political, humanitarian, and economic perspective.

Nation branding represents a much more complex type of marketing, and unlike the branding of a single person, or an organization that is made up of many key people, there are an even larger number of people who need to work tougher to constantly monitor and work hard to maintain an image that is consistent with the aim of the country. To be effective, as the literature suggests in each of the previous chapters on different brand entities, all brands must maintain control over the information used to reinforce it and respond to crises, and for a nation, these challenges are far greater than the branding of any product, service, person, or organization.

Furthermore, in light of the role that culture plays in its development, it is best to apply the general best practices of branding discussed earlier in the book while also accounting for cultural nuances that shape each country's history and values. A nation's brand is best understood through history, by examining what has been effective and what has not been effective in developing brands for different nations in the past, and apply those key findings for all re-branding efforts, which all nations ultimately will find themselves in due to the large number of uncontrollable factors that impede on this level of branding.

Endnotes

1. Moilanen and Rainisto, 2008.
2. Jansen, 2008.
3. Fan, Branding the nation: Towards a better understanding, 2010.
4. Szondi, 2007.
5. Papadopoulos and Heslop, Country equity and country branding: Problems and prospects, 2002.
6. Papadopoulos and Heslop, Product-country images: Impact and role in international marketing, 2014.
7. Fan, Branding the nation: Towards a better understanding, 2010.
8. Anholt, Anholt Nation Brands Index: How Does the World See America? 2005.
9. Garbacz-Rawson, 2007.
10. Anholt and Hildreth, Brand America: The Mother of all Brands, 2004.
11. Nye Jr., 2004.
12. Garbacz-Rawson, 2007.
13. Kitchen, Brignell, Li, and Jones, 2004.
14. Dinnie, Melewar, Seidenfuss, and Musa, 2010.
15. Dinnie, et al., 2010.
16. Kim, Shim and Dinnie, 2013.
17. Heslop, Nadeau, O'Reilly, and Armenakyan, 2013.
18. Heslop, et al., 2013.
19. Newman, 1999.
20. Newman, 1999.
21. Moorman, 2014.
22. Moorman, 2014.
23. Moorman, 2014.

CHAPTER 7

BRANDING IDEAS

INTRODUCTION

This chapter will be devoted to the application of branding strategies to ideas. Certainly one could argue that all of the previous chapters that covered the various brand entities identified in Figure 7.1 in some way relate to an idea. For example, the decision on the part of a homeowner to use energy-efficient light bulbs in every room of a house is most likely based on the specifications of this product that are identified on the package the bulb comes in, so one could argue that all products are based on some kind of ideas put forward by the manufacturer. The same holds true for services, where companies offer the consumer benefits that come in the form of benefits related to doing business with one service provider instead of another. Whether it is the choice of a doctor, lawyer, or even dry cleaner, one could make the argument that each of these service providers succeeds on the basis of their ability to convey succinctly the ideas that separate them from the competition. With this in mind, this chapter will focus on ideas that are centered on different social issues that have a high degree of complexity, and call for unique brand strategies not covered in the previous chapters. By definition, any brand can be defined as a mental entity that consists of our previous encounters with a specific product and/or service, as well as our associations and ideas about that product and/or service. If we choose specific brands, it implies that we have confidence and trust in what we buy. According to Aaker, companies have a strategic imperative to engage in active conversations with their customers, and by so doing offer a real value beyond the physical product or service that the company offers.[1]

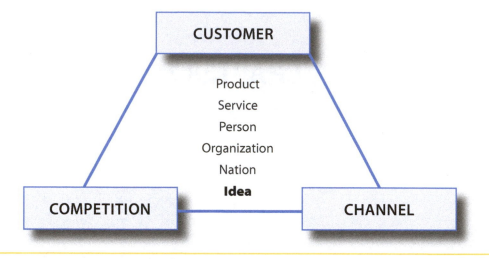

FIGURE 7.1   **Strategic Brand Focus**

Research in social marketing and corporate social responsibility (CSR) have acknowledged the necessity of addressing specific social concerns.[2] The "triple bottom line" approach—which focuses on addressing social, environmental, and economic concerns—emphasizes the different converging issues that businesses, nongovernmental, and governmental organizations may address in their branding strategy.

As discussed in the various branding entities explored throughout this book, addressing these different issues provides businesses and organizations with long-term growth and customer loyalty. For instance, consumers often use brands as a way to construct, sustain, and communicate their group identity.[3] According to a global study by Roper ASW, 38 percent of its sample of the world's consumers say, "it is very important in their decision-making that brands and companies make efforts to address social issues or causes."

It is not only businesses and organizations that develop branding initiatives around social issues, but increasingly many governments around the world recognize the importance of integrating social issues into their own countries image, especially campaigns focused on sustainability.[4] In partnership with nongovernmental organizations as well as businesses, governments can deliver on their brand promise by gaining a deeper understanding of their target audience (See Chapter 6 on Branding of Nations). For that matter, political leaders themselves are defining and crafting their brand around activities that relate to social issues. President Abdel-Fettah el-Sissi of Egypt embarked on a very nontraditional, but effective branding strategy of his own image by responding to the many social issues facing his country. As part of this effort, he engaged in a public relations campaign where he sits before audiences for hours and lets them raise social issues of concern to them, and he then responds immediately with action plans. For example, when one citizen complained about the police shutting down his food cart because he did not have a proper license, the president responded by promising to start a program to license food carts in public squares. This is a leader who was referred to in a newspaper article as, "Egypt's president ensures unique brand seen all over."[5]

Yet, the strategies that different businesses and organizations use to affect the behavior and/or opinion of their customer base may differ depending on the product or service that they are selling or the marketplace that they are operating within. As discussed in previous chapters, this ranges from the development of brand strategy around corporations, nonprofits, goods, services, political candidates, nations, or, as the focus of this chapter, ideas that center on social issues, including public health and the environment.

BRANDING AND THE CONSUMER

Scholars have segmented the social consumer benefits of a specific brand into three categories: functional, experiential, and symbolic.[6] *Functional benefits* of a specific brand refer to the performance of a product or service in addressing a certain social problem, for example in the social branding realm, environmental pollution. The *experiential benefit* refers to the feeling and emotions a consumer experiences when they use a specific brand, such that their consumer satisfaction increases knowing that the brand is addressing a social objective. Finally, the *symbolic benefit* of a brand refers to the ability of a brand to project one's self-image, as well as communicates to themselves and others the type of person that they are or the type of person that they want to be.

While these benefits are not necessarily mutually exclusive, consumers may choose one brand over another due to one of these benefits being more salient. For example, the decision to purchase a certain product or service may be driven by how one perceives its experiential and/or symbolic benefit, but the consumer is less aware of its functional benefits. Likewise, consumers may perceive these benefits differently depending on the intentions of the company to incorporate social objectives with its products.[7]

However, not all social issues are perceived the same way among the public. Social issues are embedded with values, often which make branding strategy and strategic communication more complex. For instance, Hirschman describes how our predispositions are the result of the various subgroups that we ascribe to, and that these predispositions influence what brands we are attracted to.[8] Therefore, following the strategic 3C brand framework previously mentioned, it is important to not only understand the way in which your target audience thinks about a specific social issue, including commonly held values and beliefs, but also the different ways in which your audience interacts with the brand, such as who is communicating, what channels are used to receive the communication, as well as what are the competing businesses and organizations.

REVIEW OF SUCCESSFUL SOCIAL BRANDING CAMPAIGNS

A review of the literature in social marketing reveals that many of the most successful social marketing campaigns involve businesses or organizations focusing on issues of public health and sustainability. For example, a number of businesses and organizations see the benefits of focusing on sustainable practices in driving their performance, making corporate social responsibility integral to their organizational strategy. This strategy is typically implemented when searching for marketing competitive advantages across a variety of industries.[9] Consider the example of Whole Foods Market, where social issues are fundamental to their competitive edge in food retailing. Not only does the company aim to sell organic, natural, and healthy foods, but they also emphasize purchasing from local farmers, as well as a commitment to socially drive operating practice beyond sourcing, including purchasing renewable energy for their electricity use, as well as converting their vehicles to run entirely on biofuel.[10] While Whole Foods does command premium prices, nearly every aspect of its value chain reinforces its social dimension, thus providing a unique competitive edge in the food retailing marketplace.

What is evident across examples of successful social marketing campaigns is that businesses and organizations deliver value to their customers when they deliver on their brand promise. For example, if an organization has dedicated itself to protecting the environment, consumers want evidence that the organization is following through on the promise. In today's information-rich environment, organizations can communicate this via social media, but consumers also have access to information to hold these groups accountable. Likewise, businesses that brand themselves around social causes, for example TOMS Shoes or the online eyeglasses retailer Warby Parker, need to reinforce to their customers that they are following through on their social commitment.

This in turn reinforces and sustains the consumer's desire for the brand, thus developing brand equity.

Across a range of strategic branding campaigns, businesses and organizations significantly influenced the perceptions and behavior of their customer base, which is another form of social issue marketing.[11] These branding campaigns communicate ideas both explicitly and implicitly, influencing customer behavior. For example, Charry examined the role of product placement in the child- and pre-adolescent oriented media.[12] The author discovered that bimodal audio-visual TV placements are an effective education tool for pre-adolescents, who were more likely to choose a healthy snack after they were exposed to both audio and video messages. The study supports the idea that placement of health-related messages in TV shows can effectively influence behavior and attitudes of pre-adolescents, with the main reason attributed to the fact that pre-adolescents aspire to TV characters and their lifestyles.

Miller examined the effects of the famous "Got Milk" national campaign that was launched approximately twenty years ago.[13] The campaign—which included around 300 celebrities—encouraged milk consumption as well as worked to deter young people from drinking unhealthy sugary drinks. According to Lapowsky, the campaign was extremely successful due to its simple and memorable slogan, its use of motivational messages, its humor and wit, and its ability to leverage different platforms that reached many consumers.[14] In effect, the campaign shifted the behavior of viewers to choose healthier beverage options through its widely successful execution of the campaign.

In another study, Detsiny describes how in the modern marketplace, companies need to act responsibly and represent the best interests of the consumer.[15] As such, to develop effective marketing campaigns it is important to understand the consumer as well as societal trends and dynamics, such as culturally held perceptions of gender roles and family values. Along those lines, Vargas explored how food brands address the obesity problem in Mexico. According to the article, government restrictions for advertising of soft drinks and high-calorie food are becoming tougher.[16] The author emphasizes that companies need to understand that family values and the role of women in Mexico is changing and that there is an untapped potential in the young Mexican population that companies can successfully use. In this example, the success of the message was well received because it was presented in a way that was relevant and impactful given that it was aligned with cultural values and norms for this particular group.

As these examples demonstrate, branding strategies that focus on the use of positive archetypes have a powerful effect on consumer behavior and societal outcomes.

However, branding strategies that orient around positive archetypes are not always successful in achieving certain social objectives. Reid, Baird, Bailie, and Lyle, for example, found that negative emotional appeals were most effective in reducing drunk driving instances in their study of 17–24-year-old males in Northern Ireland.[17] The authors found that condoning the behavior of an archetype as socially and personally shameful was considered the most effective branding campaign for their campaign moving forward. Thus, cultural differences must be taken into account.

While the effect of positive archetypes or the promotion of adverse consequences used in branding strategies may be influential in achieving certain social objectives, it may also be the case that the effect of these specific strategies are diminished due to what is known as the "third person effect."[18] The third person effect hypothesizes that individuals believe that mediated messages have a greater effect on others than on themselves. For example, individuals assume that they are not as susceptible to health warnings as are other people, oftentimes disregarding these warnings. Therefore, as individuals assume that they are not suggestible, this leads to reluctance to change their behavior. As a result, when it comes to strategic branding centered around social issues and behavior change, the mere presence of advertisements suggesting behavior change may have adverse results.

Online media, including social media, plays an important role in how businesses and organizations develop as well as maintain their brand strategy. Through the growth of social media and the ease by which individuals have access to information, consumers are now able to evaluate a business or organization's performance in real-time, and in so doing, businesses and organizations must work to develop and sustain that trust.[19] For example, according to Offerpop, a social marketing platform, the most effective brands focused on environmental sustainability "not only raise awareness for causes on multiple networks, but tailor their campaigns to leverage the visual web and user generated content by allowing users to submit conscious content, give back and gain exclusive information." Likewise, ComRes, a polling and research consultancy, assessed the online presence of The Grantham Institute on Climate Change, an organization that assists governments in policy-making and communication with the public. The firm developed a research taxonomy to understand online trust and sentiments of the stakeholders who visit the Institute's website. The Grantham Institute found that a company's online interaction with interested parties is critical to maintaining an identity or what else is needed in addressing the branding campaign. The Institute conducted a comprehensive study to evaluate the quality of online interactions and engagement that the high-level stakeholders have when they use the website of the

Grantham Institute on Climate Change. According to their research, website functionality has a direct impact on brand.[20]

Similarly, Newman, Howlett, Burton, Kozup, and Heintz examined how environmentally focused messages in the media can influence consumer's purchasing behavior and their choice of products.[21] The authors found that the concept of product sustainability still remains vague for many customers, and the sustainability of a product is important for customers only in specific contexts. For example, when purchasing food products, consumers place a higher value on taste and price rather than sustainability. Likewise, when purchasing an automobile, sustainability considerations are less important to the consumer than safety and performance. However, in other consumer purchasing contexts, such as household cleaning products, sustainability considerations are more important. In two separate experiments conducted to assess positive and negative product messages centered on sustainability, the authors concluded that the promotion of the consequences of not acting had a greater impact on sustainable consumer intentions than the consequences of acting. Therefore, the results from this study find that consumers are more likely to respond to reactive rather than proactive approaches to sustainable behavior.

Bissell and Rask explored the effects of media on the perceptions of beauty in women. The authors analyzed behavioral effects of body-focused ads featuring average-size women instead of unrealistic images of extremely thin models. According to the research, women were found engaging in comparisons of their own bodies and the body types of models in ads, which produced a feeling of discrepancy in women. Their results showed that average-size models in ads can help decrease anxiety in women with eating disorders, leading the authors to point to the danger of unrealistic body images in advertising, thus encouraging companies to use more realistic models to prevent the negative effect of the unrealistic beauty ideals.[22] The authors reference the "Dove Campaign for Real Beauty" as an iconic example of the new approach that has a distinct impact on beauty perceptions in society.

In another example, a public health campaign launched in 2014 by the Ontario Ministry of Health to reduce tobacco used targeted social smokers—as opposed to heavy smokers—and branded their campaign and strategic communications around this audience. The campaign's rationale was that it is much easier to help light smokers quit the addiction instead of unsuccessfully targeting heavy smokers. The objective of the campaign was to create a debate around this topic and shift thinking of "social smoking" as an acceptable behavior. In an effort to brand smoking as socially unacceptable, the authors created a social campaign that reached the target audience with both online and off-line presences, and significantly impacted public perception around the issue.

As the example above illustrates, it is important to develop a target audience and find the appropriate channels by which to communicate with that audience. However sometimes this does not always work out as planned. For instance, Rummel describes a campaign by the Roman Catholic Church in the Archdiocese of New York to create awareness of priesthood and attract more young men to consider becoming priests.[23] The church's goal was to raise awareness of priesthood among young Catholic men; however, this proved to be challenging, as a lot of young men in the area were more attracted to the secular values of the modern society. In their campaign, the Catholic Church in the Archdiocese of New York targeted young Catholic men and their parents in New York. The campaign used ads in certain print sources, such as the weekly Catholic News and local newspapers, and featured life stories of successful Catholic priests. As a result, the campaign produced some influence among religious parents, who were readers of the paper, but the effect on young Catholic men, who were the target audience, was insignificant. Given the incorrect selection of channel according to the 3C model, this campaign failed in its efforts to reach the appropriate audience.

BRANDING OF CONTENTIOUS ISSUES: CLIMATE CHANGE AND GENETICALLY MODIFIED FOODS

While the review of the literature reveals a number of social issues that businesses and organizations use for their branding strategy, we will now turn to examining two examples of social issues that differ from the others that are discussed in this chapter: climate change and genetically modified foods. These issues differ because unlike branding strategies around public health campaigns, for example, these issues are contentious, often evoking strongly held values and beliefs both among proponents and opponents.

The first issue, climate change, is one of the most politically polarizing social issues in the U.S. as well as internationally. Yet, increasingly the issue of climate change is a central focus of branding strategy among businesses and organizations around the world. The other issue we focus on, genetically modified foods (GMOs), has garnered increased attention among consumers as food producers as well as restaurants choose to voluntarily label their foods as "GMO free" or "Non-GMO." This is despite the consensus among the Food and Drug Administration and the American Medical Association that GMOs do not pose any risk to human health. Nonetheless, industry backed groups continue to fight measures that would make GMO labeling mandatory. Each of these issues, climate change and genetically modified foods, will be used to understand the way in which businesses and organizations develop their branding campaigns.

CASE STUDIES OF IDEA BRANDING

Case 1: Climate Change

To begin, within the U.S., the public overall tends to rank climate change at the very bottom of the list of the most pressing issues facing the country.[24] This is despite the fact that scientists around the world warn of the risks posed by a changing climate, the necessity to take actions to mitigate the drivers of climate change, as well as measures to adapt to a changing climate.

Moreover, within the U.S. the issue of climate change, like issues such as abortion or gun control, have developed into social identity markers where one's opinion on the issue is a reflection of his or her politics and worldview.[25] According to McCright and Dunlap, political affiliation of the U.S. public plays an important role in how citizens receive climate change messages.[26] More specifically, liberals and Democrats tend to demonstrate more concern on climate change than conservatives and Republicans.

However, we can begin to see the importance of a branding strategy just by examining whether the phenomenon is referred to as "climate change" or "global warming." While climate change and global warming are often used interchangeably, they each have a significant influence on how the issue is perceived by members of the public. Most scientists would agree that climate change is a more appropriate term due to the fact that a changing climate has many effects besides from warming, including rainfall patterns or rising sea levels. Yet the terms climate change and global warming evoke different mental images to members of the public.[27] As a result, many environmental groups tend to use the term global warming, as it is perceived with more urgency than the term climate change. Likewise, many climate change denial organizations choose to use the term global warming, as it provides an effective straw man anytime temperatures are cooler than expected.

However, regardless of the role of politics or values, the issue of environmental sensitivity is becoming a more prominent branding strategy among businesses and organizations, both in the U.S. as well as globally. In fact, it is hard to think of any businesses today that are not taking measures to reduce their ecological impact, and it is also becoming more common to see businesses taking actions to combat climate change either directly or indirectly, such as reducing energy use and relying on more sustainable supply chains. In turn, companies advertise these actions to brand themselves as environmentally conscious because they understand the importance of the issue to the general public, and hence leverage climate change as part of their overall branding strategy. For example, Kimberly Clark holds several paper based products as part of its brand portfolio, ranging from toilet paper to feminine care products to Kleenex. While the products themselves aren't exactly environmentally friendly, they are necessary, everyday products consumed in large quantities. To appeal to the environmentally sensitive consumers, Kimberly Clark has launched a sustainability initiative, running campaigns centered around environmental conservation. Their Scott and Cottonelle toilet paper brands for example recently launched a core-less toilet paper product, which removes the cardboard typically found in the center of a roll of toilet paper and reduced the environmental harm of making this product by eliminating the cardboard waste. Innovation through sustainability helps differentiate these toilet paper brands to an environmentally conscious consumer because most other brands are more wasteful in their toilet paper products, and hence Kimberly Clark effectively leveraged their sustainability marketing to the company's advantage through this product extension.

A brief look at the corporate mission statements from some of the largest global companies suggests just how important the issue of climate change is to their mission. For example, the corporate statement of Starbucks acknowledges efforts to reduce their carbon footprint as well as their initiatives to help mitigate the effects felt by farmers:

> "Climates are changing, especially in the sensitive bioregions where coffee is grown. To better understand the impact to farming communities and our supply chain, we work with Conservation International (CI) and farmers in three unique coffee-producing communities. Together we are working to identify and test effective strategies for improving the sustainability of coffee production processes, the conservation and restoration of natural habitat and opportunities to facilitate farmer access to forest carbon markets or other payment for environmental services. We have learned that each country requires differing models in order to be successful impacting farmers, and we are now working

to identify how best to share this information and involve the right organizations that can sustain the positive impact."[28]

Similarly, the Ford Motor Company discusses atmospheric contamination levels that they look to meet in their corporate statement:

"Our climate change strategy is based on doing our share to stabilize carbon dioxide (CO2) concentrations in the atmosphere at 450 parts per million (ppm), the level that many scientists, businesses, and governmental agencies believe may avoid the most serious effects of climate change."[29]

In addition, there are numerous nongovernmental organizations that are dedicated to taking action on climate change. While these organizations are not selling a specific product, they do provide a service to the individuals that donate to their cause, such as advocating for specific policies. These organizations therefore need to develop a brand strategy that communicates to their audience, or customers, that they are following through on their mission. While oftentimes these organizations are working toward the same or similar social goals, there is no doubt that these organizations use branding strategy as a way to segment themselves from other environmental organizations. As such, these organizations use climate change and the various policies that they support as a way to develop that brand.

Legacy environmental organizations such as the Sierra Club, Environmental Defense Fund, and Greenpeace, are all examples of such organizations that prioritize sustainability. However, individuals who are concerned about climate change might have different attitudes toward what is the most effective way to bring about desired change. Environmental organizations therefore take advantage of this segmentation by advocating for a specific set of policies. As such, the mission statement of the Environmental Defense Fund suggests that they work closely with members of Congress and other Washington "insiders" while advocating for more pragmatic approaches:

"We work to solve the most critical environmental problems facing the planet. This has drawn us to areas that span the biosphere: climate, oceans, ecosystems and health. Since these topics are intertwined, our solutions take a multidisciplinary approach. We work in concert with other organizations—as well as with business, government and communities—and avoid duplicating work already being done effectively by others."[30]

On the other hand, Greenpeace, according to their mission statement, may use channels outside of politics to effect change, such as promoting large-scale demonstrations, as well as powerful advertising campaigns:

> "Greenpeace is an independent campaigning organization, which uses non-violent, creative confrontation to expose global environmental problems, and to force the solutions which are essential to a green and peaceful future."[31]

Regardless of specific political affiliation, the general public views environmental impact as at least somewhat necessary, creating the shift in corporate marketing to focus on sustainability as part of their brand identity in some capacity. Brands will continue to adopt various forms of environmental consciousness in their messages, regardless of the specific product or service they provide simply because it is a critical issue internationally, and will continue to gain traction as further research is conducted and published on the issue.

Case 2: Genetically Modified Foods

Similar to climate change, businesses and organizations are increasingly seeing a branding opportunity in relation to genetically modified foods (GMOs). According to the World Health Organization, "Genetically modified foods are foods derived from organisms whose genetic material (DNA) has been modified in a way that does not occur naturally." While society has been genetically modifying different agricultural crops for centuries, the notion that large agricultural corporations are modifying many of the foods that we consume has a majority of the public concerned. As such, despite low levels of knowledge of what "genetically modified" actually means, 57 percent of the U.S. public, when asked, would avoid eating genetically modified foods and find that they are unsafe to eat.[32] This is despite the statements from leading scientific organizations around the world that consuming genetically modified foods does not pose any risk to human health.

Due to the significant negative perception of genetically modified foods in the U.S., some scholars argue that in order to correct for this "misperceived risk," the product characteristics and benefits must be marketed and thus communicated more effectively.[33] For example, proponents of genetically modified foods often choose to frame their benefits in terms of meeting rising food demands or, in technical terms, as to not garner as much media attention.[34]

Yet, due to the ethical considerations that drive consumer perceptions of genetically modified foods, such as aversion to industrial food production, attempts at communicating benefits might not be effective. Nonetheless, food producers and marketers see a promising branding strategy in labeling their products as "non-GMO," despite the fact that neither the USDA, FDA, or any other government regulatory agency is mandated to oversee this labeling process. As a result, these labels, such as the "Non-GMO Product," are nonprofit organizations who food producers pay to have their label put on their products.

The strong aversion to GMOs felt by the public suggests that in relation to GMO foods, consumers can be segmented into two main groups: risk averse consumers who are willing to pay a higher price for non-GMO foods, and the price conscious consumers who will choose conventional produce and other food products regardless of its source, and are therefore less opposed to foods containing GMOs.[35]

Restaurants have also taken advantage of the large segment of the public who is willing to pay higher prices for non-GMO foods. In April 2015, the "fast, casual" Mexican restaurant chain, Chipotle, launched their "G-M-Over It" campaign, in which they phased out all GMO products from their supply chain. This was a major marketing initiative across all of their restaurants, and a large segment of their consumers applauded their decision. Yet many saw this campaign as deceptive, given that the livestock used in their meat and dairy products were fed a GMO-inclusive diet. This led to a PR scandal and even prompted one group in California to file a lawsuit against Chipotle in 2015.

As the examples of climate change and genetically modified foods illustrate, social issues that evoke strong feelings from consumers have both significant benefits but also costs. Unlike the branding strategies around products or services, where consumers may not have strong latent values associated with a particular brand, social issues evoke strong feelings from the public that must be approached from a branding perspective with campaigns that center on the ideas that connect with peoples' emotions. As such, there is a dedicated segment of the public who cares deeply about these issues and are both willing to pay more and/or support a business or organization that shares their value system. However, when a business or organization attempts to use these issues as a core component of their brand strategy, it may produce unintended results, such as members of the public who view the initiative as deceptive. In turn, these issues present a branding initiative that relies on both how the business or organization communicates to their customers, but also how their consumers shape and construct their brand image in other public spheres, such as social media.

A STRATEGIC BRAND FOCUS

With respect to the strategic brand focus framework put forward throughout this book, the branding of ideas presents some unique differences in comparison to the other categories described in previous chapters. For instance, businesses and organizations are taking important steps to address some of the most pressing issues facing the world, including addressing the risks posed by climate change as well as improving public health and global economic conditions. Oftentimes there is little contention around these issues, for example reducing under-age drinking or promoting public health outcomes, but other cases are more contentious, such as is the case with climate change or genetically modified foods. Therefore, understanding the unique way in which consumers are influenced by the growth of communication channels as well as competition is increasingly important for developing branding strategy around social issues.

As it was described in several of the examples provided in this chapter, it is not sufficient to only understand the value and beliefs of your audience, but it is also necessary to determine the best ways to communicate to them. This notion is growing more complicated with the growth of digital media, including social media and blogs. For example, the public has greater ease with social media to re-construct how a business or organization defines their brand strategy around social issues. Having an active online presence that is bi-directional, therefore, is an important way to communicate with your target audience. Yet even a basic understanding of the sources in which your target audience gets the majority of their news and information is important, as was illustrated in the example of the Archdiocese of New York trying to recruit new priests.

In addition to the relationship between customer and channel, it is also important to examine the relationship between customer and competition within the context of branding social issues. As was apparent with the case of Chipotle and their decision to run the "G-M-Over It" campaign, the restaurant saw using the case of genetically modified foods as a way to segment themselves from other restaurants that they compete with. Yet, the long-term impact on the campaign was not all positive, as many saw this move as misleading. Moreover, one of the unique characteristics of social issues is that competition does not always come from competing businesses or organizations who are trying to capitalize on a certain segment of the public, but it may also come from outside voices who see action of certain issues misleading or going against their own individual values and beliefs. With the ease by which these voices reach large audiences, due to social media, it is important that businesses and organizations rely on the appropriate public relations techniques to assuage any criticism that may come their way.

CONCLUSION

As these examples above illustrate, branding strategies around ideas that are centered on complex social issues are most successful when an audience is identified and the messaging is tailored to that audience. These issues of course are not contained in a vacuum; social pressures, norms, and other factors influence both the credibility of the evidence and likelihood of adopting behavior change. One important characteristic to consider when adopting a branding strategy around social issues is gauging how members of the public view the importance of that issue.

For example, branding around certain issues, such as climate change or genetically modified foods, may be high-risk, but also high-reward. If a business or organization develops a branding campaign around these issues they may appeal to an engaged segment of the public, but in so doing, it has the potential to alienate other members of the public who do not share the same values or feel that the branding attempt is misleading. However, for other issues that may not be as high-risk, such as campaigns around lifestyle change (e.g., drinking and driving, tobacco use, etc.) in which there is a public consensus about the importance of that issue, sometimes businesses or organizations may fall short on their intended goal. For example, as the "third person effect" posits, individuals may perceive that increased media attention to certain issues decreases their own propensity to take action. Likewise, it may be the case that the communication strategy is not reaching the target audience due to not appropriately identifying the most effective communication channel.

Despite some of the challenges associated with branding ideas around social issues, these issues present a unique branding opportunity to reach specific audiences in ways that are different from the other categories described in this book. Regardless of the fact that these issues can be very abstract or overly complicated to most members of the public, they provide a unique opportunity for businesses and/or organizations to elucidate opinions and behavior from audiences based on individual's values and beliefs.

Endnotes

1. Aaker, 2014.
2. Kotler and Zaltman, 1971.
3. E. C. Hirschman, 2010.
4. Hicks, 2013.
5. Hendawi, 2017.
6. Park, Jaworski and MacInnis, 1986.
7. Newman, Gorlin and Dhar, 2014.
8. E. C. Hirschman, 2010.
9. De Bakker, Groenewegen and Den Hond, 2005.
10. Porter and Kramer, 2006.
11. Evans, Blitstein, Hersey, Renaud, and Yaroch, 2008.
12. Charry, 2014.
13. Miller, 2014.
14. Lapowsky, 2014.
15. Detsiny, 2004.
16. Vargas, 2014.
17. Reid, Baird, Bailie, and Lyle, 2002.
18. Innes and Zeitz, 1988.
19. Francis, 2011.
20. ComRes and the Grantham Institute on Climate Change and the Environment: Increasing digital influence over the climate change debate, 2014.
21. Newman, Howlett, Burton, Kozup, and Heintz, 2012.
22. Bissell and Rask, 2010.
23. Rummel, 2000.
24. Gallup, 2016.
25. Nisbet, 2011.
26. McCright and Dunlap, 2011.
27. Whitmarsh, 2009.
28. Starbucks Corporation, 2017.
29. Ford Motor Company, 2017.
30. Environmental Defense Fund, 2017.
31. Greenpeace, 2017.
32. Funk and Raine, 2016.
33. Bredahl, 1999.
34. Nisbet and Newman, Framing, the Media, and Environmental Communication, 2015.
35. Baker and Burnham, 2001.

CHAPTER 8

BEST PRACTICES

INTRODUCTION

Consumer preferences and behaviors are changing. During the 1990s and 2000s, consumers were happy to let everyone know what branded products they were using, whether it was on clothing, an automobile, or any other type of product that sent a message to others about their personal tastes and desires. However, since that time, consumers are moving in a slightly different direction, preferring, for example, to wear clothing without any label on them for others to see, which as one might suspect, is having an impact on companies that for many years were used to promoting their products with flashy logos. For some retailers, like Abercrombie & Fitch, it has prompted them to engage in new strategies to de-emphasize their bold brands, resulting in a new logo to alter their image for their clothing line due to changing consumer preferences. There are others who argue that luxury shoppers prefer more subtle branding, and that they already know when they see an expensive product by its design and other features, so it is not necessary to "shout-it-out" with a bold logo. Who can forget the little green crocodile that could be found on the shirts of Lacoste shirts in the 1980s, or other featured animals like ponies, marlins, and moose on other well-known companies' shirts.[1]

The branding lessons reported in this book are based on the best practices used by a wide cross-section of people and organizations to create a unique representation for their particular brand in a given marketplace. The main argument put forward in this book is that a brand is more than just a logo, such as a little green crocodile, or a visual representation of a product, but can include a very broad collection of entities that all rely on the same key marketing principle, which is the importance of defining what it is you sell and pointing out its strengths and unique features that make it different from your competition. The ability to carry out this task relies on both a key understanding of your customer, as well as the know-how to communicate this information through the proper media and distribution channels. We have introduced the Strategic Brand Focus, which puts forward the 3 C's: Customer, Competition, and Channel. Through an understanding of these three key factors that exist for any brand, a person, or organization is better equipped to succeed in their respective marketplaces.

The other significant contribution of the book lies in the innovative approach that was used to define exactly what a brand is. Each of Chapters 2 through 7 define the concept of a brand for six different entities: products, services, people, organizations, nations, and ideas. In each of the chapters that cover these different brand entities, it became clear that there were certain characteristics that worked better for some and not for others. For example, as a company seeks to brand a product, it has the benefit of working with a tangible item, easily identified in the minds of the consumer, like a can of Coca-Cola. On the other hand, for those organizations that are in the business of trying to convince the world that climate change is real and is impacted by man, the task becomes more complicated as there are many different scientific dimensions to the argument that are not easily laid out for a citizen of a country to understand.

In a sense, as one moves from branding a simple product at one extreme to a complicated idea like climate change at the other extreme, the branding challenge is more difficult as a result of the communication channels that are used, and the high level of interference from competing sources to get their message across. For Coca-Cola, the competition is more easily defined, and will more than likely include other companies selling similar sodas or alternative drinks that may be consumed by the same customer. However, for an organization like 350.org, Greenpeace, or the Sierra Club, all of whom are trying to take action to unite other climate activists into a movement, and combat the risks posed by climate change, it is a more difficult task to identify your competition, although it is still possible. Needless to say, the best branding practices for these organizations will be very different than for the Coca-Cola Corporation. Along with the unique branding challenge that comes with choosing the correct communication channel lies the important task of defining exactly who your customer is. For a product like Coca-Cola, it is much easier to carry out marketing and consumer research to define the needs satisfied, such as the demographic and lifestyle profile of key customer segments, as opposed to compiling a profile of climate change supporters, thus further complicating the branding task in this domain.

Or take the case of the 2017 NCAA champions, the North Carolina Tar Heels. This is a great example of successful branding by one of the great sports teams, led by one of the great basketball coaches of all time, Roy Williams. The 2017 NCAA championship game played between the North Carolina Tar Heels and the Gonzaga Bulldogs pitted one of the most successful brands in all of sports against what many referred to as the "Cinderella" team of all college teams competing. The Bulldogs represented the antithesis of a well branded team: a school that never before made it to the Final Four, competing with one of the most famous college basketball teams, under the leadership of one of the most famous college basketball coaches, Roy Williams, already inducted into the Hall of Fame. The Tar Heels came into the tournament with five national titles, needless to say, all of this added up to a very competitive challenge to the Bulldogs. It is very difficult to beat a team that has a brand that has been so well developed over many years with a number of successes to its name. Perhaps the one branding technique that gave Gonzaga some equal press time to promote their "team" brand was the "personal" brand of their star center, a 7-foot-1 player from Poland, Przemek Karnowski, who sported a beard almost as noticeable as his body size. By leveraging their star in multiple media venues, including social media, television, and with posters, they were effective at taking his personal brand and extending it to the team. This is a case of an organization getting branded by one of its most successful products, and using that as part of their psychological arsenal against a very well experienced organization, the North Carolina Tar Heels.[2]

THE ROLE OF BRANDING IN MARKETING

In Chapter 1 we defined a brand as the essence of a product, service, idea, person, organization, or nation that conveys meaning on multiple levels to different segments of people. Branding involves the process of creating a name, image, and logo that distinguishes and separates an entity from competitors that defines it and makes it possible to stand out as unique and different in the minds of people. A powerful brand strategy gives you a noteworthy edge in increasingly aggressive markets. Essentially, a brand is your promise to your client. It lets them know what they can expect from you, what value you bring, and how others perceive you.

The role of branding is becoming increasingly important today, and in a rapidly evolving digital world saturated with social media, news outlets, and interactive engagement, new marketing channels are shifting the way brands interact with their audiences. This is further complicated by the movement toward online channels that don't afford a company the opportunity to connect with their customer in a face-to-face situation. Along with staying current on the ever-evolving digital landscape, brands must continuously innovate to reach and build strong connections with their audiences. The traditional face-to-face interaction between brand and consumer is rapidly declining, if already not obsolete for certain brands, and thus it is imperative for brands to correctly navigate this to stay competitive. However, companies still need to connect with their desired audience on an emotional level, which can only happen if they are constantly monitoring customer preferences and desires.

Ultimately, any brand, whether it is a personal brand for an up-and-coming millennial, or an established brand for a company that exists in multiple markets, must reinforce a loyalty among its followers. The phenomenon of brand love was introduced as a way to maintain a brand loyal following, and this means going beyond just liking a brand. It extends to the idea that a brand must be exclusive in some way, and at the same time connects to a community of others who feel the same way about it. As previously discussed in Chapter 1, there must be a sense of community as an antecedent of brand loyalty before brand love can be achieved. This sense of community can happen in several different ways, but some of the more effective ones are through cultivating these influencers and/or sponsorships. Brands that provide a sense of community and self-enhancement are likely to produce brand love. Brand lifestyles are also an effective way to strengthen brand community and brand identification.

The fact remains that branding plays a key role in all marketing decisions, and effectively becomes the starting point at which a person, organization, or nation can develop a marketing plan to carry out the stated goals. As was evident in the previous chapters for each of the entities analyzed, before a brand identity can be established, there needs to be a careful analysis of who the target of the branding strategy is (as highlighted in the Customer branch of the 3C model). This information then allows for an organization to determine other important business decisions, including level of sales that can be expected; necessary production goals to respond to expected sales; determination of how products can be delivered in an efficient and effective manner; and in the long run, as a pre-cursor to the management of the relationship with the customer.

Whereas the best practices for branding across the different entity types discussed in the book may be unique as was established in Chapters 2 through 7, they may have certain common characteristics, summarized in the 3C model through the three key aspects of branding: Customer, Competition, and Channel. The model essentially consolidates the best practices for each brand entity that was highlighted in each respective chapter, and any brand strategy must incorporate them. By putting a stronger focus on those marketing components that are incorporated into the Strategic Brand Focus, the point was made that branding strategies must be thought about in a new way for all marketers, and that there exists in different markets, depending on the vantage point one takes.

The most effective way to isolate the various best practices for different entity types is to consider the many different organizational structures that have to be accounted for across the brand entities, and the subtle nuances that exist when it comes to defining the customer, accounting for the competition, and then choosing the correct channels to use to communicate and distribute the product, service, or idea successfully. We all live in a world of brands, whether it is our career, or a cause of importance to us, or a political ideology that appeals to each of us, and for each to succeed, marketing strategies must be used that take into account the conclusions drawn in this book

One of the key objectives of all branding is to bring about behavior change, but as it is well known in marketing circles, this usually must be preceded by changes in the way people think about a product, service, or any other entity in question. It is not sufficient just to educate people about a given brand, but it is imperative to persuade them before a change in behavior is possible. A brand is a multi-faceted construct that includes a wide range of meanings to different people in different sectors of society. In some sectors, brand boils down to the emotional connection made between a buyer and a seller, and without a strong emotional connection with your customers, whether it is a citizen, user, or payer for your product or service, voter, or even some other organization you are trying to connect with, the organization you represent will not be successful. A brand can also include bundles of meaning which allows it to be part of myth markets. Some have argued that information/cognition and emotion only tell part of the story about brands, especially when it comes to some areas like climate change, and that meaning plays a far larger role in the branding process.

A brand can also pertain to a nation, such as Russia, whose leader is seeking to define his country in the minds of people around the world. It is a deeply complex exercise from a marketing vantage point to arrive at a brand concept for Russia that will communicate the culture, values, and characteristics of the Russian people to others all around the world. Specifically, one has to begin to wonder how Vladimir Putin, the president of Russia, has used branding to elevate the status of his country from a second-tier nation (in terms of military and economic strength), to one that has been at the center of controversies and debate that puts him and his country in the news on a regular basis.

For some product marketers, a brand identity can be created by something as simple as a very small image. For example, emojis are tiny images of animals and other objects like faces that are inserted in digital conversations, primarily through social media and text message conversations. These are not to be confused with what many refer to as logos, but in light of the fact that many companies use similar objects as a logo, such as Polo shirts with the very small polo player on a horse, one could easily confuse them. This raises the interesting comparison of emojis with the logos of companies that are used to define their brands. In a similar way, emojis are used by people communicating with one another to define an emotion, thought, or expression that encapsulates that in a single image. In Japan, where emojis were developed, the use of these symbols can have many different meanings, such as the surfer, which can suggest that a sender of a digital communication wants to break up, meaning they want to "surf" out of their relationship. However, in the U.S., the use of a surfer would not have that same meaning. This brings us to the very important role that brand plays, and how it can be perceived very differently between two people, let alone two people who live in different countries in the world. However, for those very well-known logos, such as the golden arches of McDonalds, there is a universal meaning that is conveyed with it, and that is a representation of a restaurant. No, a logo is not what branding is all about, however, it is used to identify, communicate, and express how a particular entity seeks to separate itself from other competitive brands in a market.[3]

STRATEGIC BRAND FOCUS

The 3C model presents a comprehensive analysis of the different roles that brand plays across a wide range of entities, connecting both the common and unique aspects that branding plays in a manner that has never before been addressed. By using a strategic brand focus, individuals and organizations can ensure that they will be able to build the strongest possible brand, making them competitive and standing out in the minds of their customers. This approach to branding also enables those organizations seeking to alter public opinion, whether it is a political leader of a nation trying to create a new identity with citizens; a startup trying to convince skeptics about the benefits of their innovation; or an advocacy group in the business of trying to alter existing attitudes about the mission and goals of a nonprofit organization, it is critical that a strategic orientation be used to define the identity of a brand.

Customer

In order for a brand strategy to be effective, there needs to be a clear definition of who exactly the customer is, and what their needs, wants, and desires are. The construct of the "Customer" takes on many different roles beyond that as a user of a product or service sold by a for-profit organization, and can include a whole host of other types of interested parties, depending on what the entity entails. Regardless of who the intended target of the brand is, there needs to be a careful assessment behind the best approach to use to connect with that particular audience, whether to reach them on an emotional or rational level, or whether to present the brand with a futuristic point of reference, or with a situational reference of when and how the brand can be used. All best practices start with this kind of analysis and evaluation. All organizations must engage in a process referred to as market segmentation, where the needs and wants identified in a marketplace are broken down to reflect the aggregated views of key market segments that hold the promise of a strong return on a company's resources if they focus their brand on the basis of a unique set of needs and wants. There is no end to the level at which an organization can break down a market into segments, and this is the key point behind any branding strategy, and that is to determine which key segments exist, and whether each one will serve as an attractive market to target.

Competition

Beyond the analysis of the needs and wants of the customer, donor, voter, stakeholder, or whomever may have an interest in a brand, comes the realization that although a target market may exist that is interested in a branded product that has specific features that satisfies their needs, it may not be feasible for a company to develop such a product successfully if there are other companies who have greater resources, economies of scale, or sheer technological know-how that make it near impossible to market a brand that will succeed in a highly competitive marketplace. This brings to light the importance of positioning a brand in a crowded market so that it stands out as an option that has a competitive advantage over other brands that seek to get the attention of a similar audience. Every brand needs to stand out from the competition, and a deep understanding of target market needs should drive brand differentiation strategies.

Channel

The last of the 3 C's is the choice of channels that are used to implement a successful branding strategy. This of course ties into the unique characteristics of the group or person seeking to create the brand identity that allows it to leverage its strengths and experiences as it relates to the brand in question. It is important to have a thorough understanding of the organization or entity that is involved in the branding process, and to take into account their capability to carry off the branding strategy successfully in selected channels. Whereas all companies that seek to satisfy the needs and wants of their customers, they must operate on the principle that they must be in a position to develop the research and development processes to execute this successfully. All organizations must be involved in this kind of strategic analysis of the channels they operate in if they expect their brands to be communicated effectively in their respective marketplaces. Without a strategic brand focus, it becomes very difficult for any person, organization, or nation to be successful in their branding initiatives.

PERSONAL BRANDING

The branding of people includes public figures (politicians, celebrities, athletes, etc.), as well as all individuals who seek to identify themselves in a unique manner in their professional careers. The value of a personal brand can be witnessed as one inspects some of the greatest success stories in both the business and political sectors in society. One of the more recent success stories can be found in the Trump Organization, where the sons of Mr. Trump took advantage of their father's new fame around the world as the forty-fifth president, and leveraged his position by expanding the brand into new markets. By expanding into parts of the U.S. where their father has been embraced by his followers, especially those states where he beat Hillary Clinton, they started planning the opening up of new hotel chains.

The argument put forward in this area of branding is that human personalities are both consistent and dynamic and may have long-term, consistent traits, yet may react differently in various situations—and therefore a branding strategy for a person must remain clear and consistent. One of the central purposes and conclusions from research in this area of branding centers on the determination of why and how consumers form strong attachments to human brands. Some of the conclusions that came from the research reported on this subject are the importance of being authentic, which equates with matching your actions with your character, as well as to always make sure that you always follow through with promises. Ultimately, personal branding is effective because it helps to build trust with other people. In the ongoing process of building trust with others around you, your personal brand needs to be constantly working at building and nurturing relationships with people around you, and to reinforce the success of that process, one must be constantly engaged in reassessing their own actions to alter their vision and direction. At the same time, there was some evidence that there can be some negative side effects from engaging in this process, such as the risk of not carrying off the management of your brand in a credible manner, which includes constantly changing your image and looking almost opportunistic as you constantly respond to different events. This was found to be true in particular with CEO's or Hollywood stars who get into trouble with the law or in personal matters that reveal their lack of judgment in dealing with others, putting them on the defensive, and in the process hurting their own personal brand.

Take the case of Peter Marino, principal of Peter Marino Architect PLLC, who is not only well known because of his expertise as an accomplished architect, with offices around the world and a staff of over 150 people in his New York office, but also because of the unique personal brand he established for himself. This is an architect with many accomplishments, including the re-design of some of New York's most well-known stores and boutiques, such as the Giorgio Armani flagship store on Madison Avenue, and the winner of the French Ministry of Culture award in 2012 because of his contribution to the arts in France. If you were to view an image of Mr. Marino, it would become obvious that this is not your typical architect, dressed in a two-piece suit, but instead, someone who has a unique fashion style built around the image of tattooed biker, dressed in black clothing, laced with buckles and studs and a leather cap that makes him stand out in any crowd. The lesson here for anyone interested in establishing a successful personal brand is to set yourself apart from the competition in some unique way that makes you and your talents stand out. It may be necessary to build upon your professional success with an image that reinforces your creativity and style in a clever, but believable manner.[4]

Unlike the thinking of most people, a brand is more than just a logo or trademark, and it has more to do with just products or services, but can include many different entities. However, what may be of the greatest value of the contribution put forward by this innovative book is the way in which each and every person, regardless of what they do, or what industry they work in, is how the best practices reported can be used to express an individual's "personal brand" the way that Mr. Peter Marino has. Who would ever think that this man is a famous architect, or that he was educated at one of the most well-known academic institutions, namely the Cornell University College of Architecture, Art and Planning. Who would guess how successful he is, and that he has rubbed shoulders with some of the most wealthy and successful people around the world, helping them to design their businesses as well as their homes. The point is that his personal brand makes him stand out in a way that gives him an edge on his competition because he gets peoples' attention wherever he goes. Getting the attention of people, especially your customers, is one of the first integral steps that a company can take.

For those individuals who seek to promote their own personal brand among others for either personal or professional gain, certain rules should be followed. Whereas it is not always necessary to create a personal brand that has you standing out among the crowd of others who carry out similar professional activities as you do, it is advisable to target your image to a particular audience (e.g., co-workers, boss, etc.) that is in sync with their desired perception of someone in your position. This will force you to take into account your unique abilities and characteristics, which is a very good starting point. Personal branding is becoming very important in the United States, and comes with the notion that anyone can reach any goal if they set their mind to it.

One of the key ingredients to a successful personal brand is the understanding of the emotional connections you have with the people who you are seeking to identify with around you, whether that is co-workers, friends, or even family. It is important to understand that as a person engages with others, over time, your personal brand must be managed, in no different a way than a company manages the brand of the products they sell over time. If circumstances change, it is critical that you alter your personal brand to adapt to these changes.

CORPORATE BRANDING

As the role of technology continues to impact the branding of all products and services, there is an effort on the part of corporations to integrate top managers throughout the branding process to strategically align the various components and departments within a company. The changes taking place technologically can be found on both the product side as well as with media putting an even bigger pressure on organizations to rely on branding as a constant link between firm and customer. Brands continue to be one of the most valuable assets, and at risk for any corporation is the possibility of a well-known brand failing and destroying the reputation of the company that took many years to build in just a matter of days. The conclusions in the book on this subject suggest that many companies are taking those risks seriously and seeking ways of leveraging their brand equity, and at the same time attempting to limit their exposure to any extreme risk in a market. One of the strategies that firms are taking is to keep their corporate name separate from individual product brands.

Services are different from goods on several levels, but primarily are most different in their intangibility; services cannot be held and inspected as one would a product, which creates challenges for the corporation engaged in service branding. Furthermore, it was brought out in the chapter on services branding that there is movement toward services beginning to be delivered vis-à-vis the Internet that is the result of advances in IT. It was pointed out that this is happening in online banking phone application management, reservation/project management software, and in other area where services are shifting to less person-based and more technology-based. This calls for changes in branding strategies that were highlighted previously in this chapter, putting pressure on corporations to engage in activities that monitor how they are perceived by stakeholders, customers, and anyone who may have reason to comment about their efficiency and effectiveness as a service provider. But there still exists a large number of services that are still delivered by humans, and this calls for branding strategies that account for the important role that the person serves in the process.

Whereas the field of relationship marketing is by no means a new discovery, it does play a very important role in better understanding how to succeed as a service brander. There continues to be an important emphasis put on the relationship between service provider and receiver, making all touch points between the service provider and customer critically important. This is well documented in the hotel industry. Hotels are beginning to flood the markets with new brands, many of them catering to the millennials, and offering lifestyle options that are unique to their age cohort. The Hilton Hotel chain is opening up hotels under the new Canopy brand that are geared to consumers looking for a more "hip" boutique-style option. In fact, they even changed the titles of the employees in these new hotels to "enthusiasts" for staff, and "chief enthusiast" for the general manager of each hotel. Another new chain of branded hotels under the parent company Hilton will be a series of lower-priced boutique hotels called Tru Hotel. This movement toward new hotel brands is the result of the bigger hotel chains like Hilton and Marriott having so many properties under their current parent brand name, that they need to add new branded hotels in their effort to grow as a corporation. Executives for these big hotel chains make the point that there are only so many "Hilton" or "Marriott" hotels that can exist in a single market, and the millennials, as a segment of the consumer, are presented hotels with the need to respond to their unique and changing tastes, where they are looking for better technology in the rooms, and more interesting lobbies and restaurants.[5]

Some of the best practices for corporations operating in the service sector are suggesting a need to cultivate more direct relationships with customers, especially in light of the rapid movement in e-commerce for all organizations who are not having the same level of personal contact with their customers. This makes the brand-building process for these types of corporations that much more difficult. The service brand building process must include bringing together the relationship that exists between the organization and its employees, in addition to the relationship taking place between the customer and the corporation's employees. Research in this area shows that in order for a long-lasting relationship to exist, both the customer and the corporation need to realize that there are benefits that will result from continuing on with the relationship. Moreover, in order to deepen relationships across various channels, corporations must create effective consumer touch points. To put it another way, brands must be present and encourage the customer-brand interaction. This is particularly important in the digital space, where these interactions tend to take place across social media channels, blogs, and consumer review websites and applications like Yelp.

As it pertains to corporate branding, relationship marketing focuses on strengthening the reputation of a company in the eye of stakeholders, especially through the products and services it sells. However, these activities tend to be under-funded, and for those corporations that expect to succeed in the changing marketplace that exists today, it would be wise on their part to pay more attention to this, along with greater resources to devote to implement strategies to carry out these activities. In this digital age we live in, there is a need for more transparency, as well as streamlined integration of corporate brand messages within multinational corporations. Whereas globalization still remains a challenge for modern companies, the conclusions reported on this subject recommend that multinational companies adopt the methods of cross-functional teams in order to deliver consistent corporate messages across all of its stakeholders, local cultures, and constituents.

Since brands are so significant for the success of a modern business, it is crucial to measure the impact and manage it effectively. It is difficult to quantify the intangible value of a brand. Corporations that sell products need to know that to attract the best talent and as well as an unconditional level of customer loyalty beyond price consideration, a company needs to develop a strong corporate brand beyond the strength of individual product brands. Today, customers want to support companies that make a positive impact on society. For those companies that are successful in doing this, the brand identity of those company's products will become very attractive, leading to greater sales and revenue. It needs to be emphasized that the best practices to be carried out will very much be dependent on the particular product or service that is being marketed, and the unique characteristics of the customers the corporation is seeking to attract.

Take the case of Hennessy Corporation, where an invitation-only boutique is used to invite the best clients of LVMH Moet Hennessy Louis Vuitton in a Parisian apartment. In the elegant dining room of the apartment, Moet Hennessy's clients can spend $16,000 trying different cognacs and wines, as well as limited editions of their best champagne Dom Perignon. This is one example of a company leveraging its brand identity to attract a very unique segment of consumers, namely the top 0.1 percent of the world's richest people, slightly over 200,000 people with a net worth of over $30 million, who represent close to 20 percent of the luxury spending. Other companies have also used this same approach to appeal to a very small niche of luxury consumers, including Harrods in London, where select customers are invited for meals served by world famous chefs, to Stefano Ricci, who fly their tailor to customers around the world to make suits that can cost up to $20,000. The brand loyalty that comes to these firms from their customers is what they are seeking to reinforce. By using these extreme environments to sell their products, they hope to put them into the right mood to spend. The point here is that every company has to take advantage of their brand reputation, and work to reinforce it with this kind of marketing. Taking a closer look at the client who might walk into the Parisian apartment run by Moet Hennessy, there are the possibilities to try a wine, Chateau d'Yquem, which sells for 100,000 Euros a barrel. Or there is the sampling menu that comes along with the fine champagnes for 15,000 Euros. Every corporation seeks to reinforce their image in the minds of their customers, create a strong emotional connection with them, and this is how it is done for a very select segment of luxury consumers in the world.[6]

NONPROFIT AND POLITICAL BRANDING

Nonprofit branding is an understudied field of marketing, and can include several different brand entities as was pointed out in earlier chapters in the book, including charities, cause-oriented organizations, and nongovernmental organizations that seek to advocate on the part of a particular cause. In fact, organizations that fall under this umbrella all rely on the power of their brand identity in a market to create a movement of people who buy into their mission, such as political organizations. This is also true for those organizations that advocate a particular issue, such as 350.org or the Sierra Club, both of whom have been very active in the creation of movements to fight climate change. Finally, charitable organizations that seek to help those segments of society that need help, like the poor or abused, all use their brands to reach out to followers to perpetuate the cause.

The case of a nonprofit is a slightly different case where the organization is not necessarily selling a line of goods or services, but instead is in the business of promoting a brand identity that is more closely tied into the purpose and focus of the organization, regardless of whether it is seeking donations; requesting people to engage in a specific activity, such as protecting the environment; or seeking to advocate a particular political position in society. Whereas these are not necessarily the only types of nonprofits that operate, they do represent a type of organization that sets them apart from the corporation. In fact, it is very likely that a nonprofit will be more closely connected to a particular individual who seeks to take advantage of their notoriety in society, such as former Vice President Al Gore who has been very outspoken on the risks of climate change through his foundation, The Climate Change Reality Project, a nonprofit devoted to solving the climate crisis. The best practices in this area draw on some of the conclusions reported in the research on personal branding than on those drawn in the area of corporate product branding, but can in some cases benefit from the conclusions drawn in the service branding sector.

The research indicates that charitable organizations often apply branding frameworks from commercial branding without adjusting them to the realities of their sector. For example, it was determined that nonprofit organizations can enjoy a sustained growth when they adopt some branding techniques used in the commercial sector. However, the strategies should be adjusted to the charity organizations, with the focus centering on increasing an organization's presence in the minds of their target market, as well as to build up a stronger loyalty with them. The ultimate benefit of this results in more donations. Effective branding in the charitable sector is a more complex endeavor than one would find in the commercial marketplace, because in addition to having to respond to the needs of donors, there needs to be efforts made to influence key entities, including commercial partners, the government, and the public. This raises the importance of building trust as one of the most important tasks for these nonprofit brand managers.

Political organizations represent even another type of organization that is unique and different from corporations and nonprofit organizations because they are in the business of campaigning for office, and once elected to office, they engage in a service-related activity in the running of government. Although a political party is clearly not seeking to sell their service from a traditional perspective, they do rely on branding to connect with citizens, and need contributions (in the form of both money and manpower) from many different people and organizations to get re-elected.

Some of the best practices in this nonprofit sector come from the importance of increasing the brand-consumer interactions, where both parties derive benefit by establishing and deepening these relationships. Just as consumers want their voices to be heard, so do citizens and voters. The importance of building relationships as it pertains to political marketing offers some of the key best practices. Politicians running for office understand that in order to get elected, they must create value for the general public who holds the voting power. This can only happen if their political organization is able to establish a brand that is rooted in shared community relationships. Political organizations need to ensure that they have a firm grasp of their target market's needs, wants, values, and behaviors, and that those are aligned with the politician's own personal values and political views. Furthermore, they must be prepared to engage in crisis management, a more pressing issue in this sector where there is 24/7 news coverage of political campaigns.

For those nonprofit organizations in the business of advocating for causes, another set of best practices needs to be put into place. Conclusions in this sector reveal the importance that consumers place on the role that companies play in addressing social issues and causes. It turns out that consumers choose product and service brands on the basis of their support for causes important to them. Additionally, the most effective social marketing campaigns involve businesses or organizations focusing on issues of public health and sustainability, such as those that pay closer attention to sustainable practices in driving their performance, and make social responsibility an integral part of their overall organizational strategy.

Organizations that deliver on their brand promises are the most successful. For example, if an organization has dedicated itself to protecting the environment, consumers want evidence that the organization is following through on the promise. In the information-rich environment that all organizations operate in, especially as a result of the strong influence of social media, it is a two-way street, where interested parties can get access to information to document the performance of the organization in the same way that this can be used as a communication vehicle to announce that their promises have been delivered. In fact, it is not only nonprofit organizations that can follow these best practices, but it also holds true for corporations that are in the business of wrapping their brand around social causes, like TOMS Shoes or the online eyeglasses retailer Warby Parker, both of whom have strong commitment to various social causes.

One important characteristic to consider when adopting a branding strategy around social issues is gauging how members of the public view the importance of that issue. For example, organizations that are branding around issues such as climate change or genetically modified foods, will find themselves in a high-risk and high-reward situation. If a business or organization develops a branding campaign around these issues they may appeal to an engaged segment of the public, in so doing it has the potential to alienate other members of the public who do not share the same values or feel that the branding attempt is misleading. However, for those issues that may not be as high-risk, such as campaigns around lifestyle change (e.g., drinking and driving, tobacco use, etc.) in which there is a public consensus about the importance of that issue, sometimes businesses or organizations may fall short on their intended goal. This calls for the use of a very clear communication strategy to establish the intent and focus of the organization. The research in this area suggests that individuals may perceive that increased media attention to certain issues decreases their own propensity to take action, or it may be the case that the communication strategy is not reaching the targeted audience due to not appropriately identifying the most effective communication vehicle.

It is important that these nonprofit organizations understand the value and beliefs of their audience, and then leverage that with an active online presence that is bi-directional. In addition to the importance of the relationship between customer and channel, it is also important to examine the relationship between customer and competition within the context of branding social issues. For those corporations that choose to tie into social causes supported by nonprofit organizations, such as with the case of Chipotle and their decision to run the "G-M-Over It" campaign, the restaurant found out that it was to their benefit to use the case of genetically modified foods as a way to position themselves vis-à-vis competition. As a result of the ease by which organizations can promote their causes through social media, it is important that they rely on the appropriate public relations techniques to assuage any criticism that may be directed at them.

NATION BRANDING

Nation branding brings together much of the literature and best practices reported in the previous chapters, all of which when aggregated across the different entities covered, represent an overall impression of a nation through the products and services they sell, as well as through the individuals and organizations who represent different sectors of society that may be unique to one country, but not another. All nations represent brands at each of the different entity levels discussed in previous chapters, which when taken together, present a unified brand identity of the nation to anyone trying to understand how a country is branded. Nation branding is a widely complex level of branding which encompasses a variety of people, organizations, and political groups by which a brand reputation is formed by both the citizens of the nation as well as external groups around the world.

A nation's brand is defined by the total sum of all perceptions of the nations along various elements (including but not limited to people, place, culture/language, history, food, fashion, global brands, celebrities, etc.). Whereas a nation brand is a holistic approach to capturing the complexities and nuances of the nation's cultures, national branding refers simply to the signature product of a nation. Although these two terms appear similar, this distinction is important to note. Given the vast differences in cultural norms, traditions, and views among countries, each nation's brand is unique and hence a strategy that works for one country may not necessarily work for a different country that has different views, values, and practices.

For example, if one were to compare the US to China, each country would need to follow a unique brand strategy that accounts for the differences of the economic and political systems they each operate under. The norms and values that resonate with the American public will not be effective with the norms and values in Chinese culture, and vice versa. As a result, these two nations project very different brands, each representing their unique cultures. Hence, in nation branding, the best practices followed in one country cannot simply be applied to another nation. However, it was determined that regardless of the country, those people and organizations that seek to define their brand in the minds of people both within and outside a country's borders must take into account the aspirations and values of the targeted audience, as well as rely on the correct channels to communicate the brand identity.

Understanding a nation's brand identity as it is perceived by other international groups provides opportunity to improve or change aspects of a nation's brand in order to enhance external brand perception and reputation. Along with the external perspective, the perception of citizens of the country is equally important to consider, particularly along the lines of leadership, excitement, sophistication, tradition, and peacefulness. The combination of internal and external perceptions drives brand strategy through identifying areas of opportunity as to what aspects of the brand need to be improved or changed to reach the ideal state.

In light of the fact that nation branding is one of the most complex levels of branding because of the role culture plays in its development, it is best to apply the general best practices of branding discussed earlier in the book while also accounting for cultural nuances that shape each country's history and values. A nation's brand is best understood through history, by examining what has been effective and what has not been effective in developing brands for different nations in the past, and apply those key learnings for future re-branding efforts.

THE FUTURE OF BRANDING

Co-Creation

Co-creation is the future of branding according to some researchers.[7, 8] In fact, the notion of co-creation is bound up in one's sense of community, and as a result of the many stakeholders who may be engaged in the process, including both consumers and advocates who impact on peoples' perceptions of a product, service, or idea (such as climate change) will impact the brand identity in question.[9] According to Gobe, the modern economy is consumer-focused, and with the power of the Internet, companies can and should engage in active dialogues with the consumer.[10] More and more companies actively engage with their customers and local communities, share information, and build relationships with their fans. H-to-H (human-to-human) marketing is the term that marketing experts have recently adopted and used instead of the terms "B-to-C" (Business-to-Consumer) and "B-to-B" (Business-to-Business) marketing.[11, 12] The engagement represents both potential opportunities and expected risks, as often happens in human interactions, particularly as social media communication becomes increasingly integral in the co-creation process. However, Yan does not recommend that companies exit social media due to the risks.[13] According to Yan and others going against "transparency and oneness" when both of them are extremely valued by the public, would mean to undermine both personal and organizational brands through "appearing 'above' one's supporters."[14]

Consumer co-creation is a trend that goes beyond product innovation, and can powerfully reshape modern marketing and branding. There is an argument put forward that calls for the need for there to be a partnership between managers and employees, as well as with all of the stakeholders to create and maintain effective brands.[15, 16, 17, 18, 19, 20]

One of the most important contributions to the literature has been the work by O'Guinn and Muniz, who refer to brand communities as a crucial element of modern branding, which represents an effective way to strengthen brand identification through the concept of a brand lifestyle.[21] In addition, the authors warned marketers that their interpretations of brand meaning might be detached from the real meaning that occupies the consumer's mind. Therefore, marketing activities built on misinterpretation cannot represent a real consumer co-creation. Prahalad and Ramaswamy authored a classic work that has served as a foundation for the field of brand co-creation. The authors have proposed four elements of customer co-creation: dialogue, access, risk assessment, and transparency.[22] Other authors have followed up on their work and reinforced their findings. For example, involvement in the community and sharing of knowledge are two factors that enable co-creation, which is described as a series of "encounters" between the company and the consumers, where companies need to play an active role in seeking the interactions and motivating the consumer to share their experiences. As the result of this kind of effort, the process improves and transforms service experiences.[23]

According to Haltch and Schultz, the co-creation concept provides an ongoing dialogue and feedback on branding activities that companies receive from social networks.[24] The authors propose that dialogue, transparency, and respect are crucial in consumer engagement. Yan agreed that the need for transparency has only grown with the advance of social media. Undoubtedly, as consumers become active contributors, risks increase.[25] Gregory emphasizes the importance of shared knowledge, experience, and segmentation that need to take place to tailor the messages for each group of stakeholders.[26] Muniz and O'Guinn make the point that brand communities are founded on human relationships and transparency, and are represented by shared values that are centered around a set of commonly held moral norms.[27]

It has become very clear that co-creation, and in particular the development of communities founded on the basis of interactions between parties who have similar interests, is a fundamental concept that is driving the world of politics, including electoral campaigns as well as those issues like climate change and genetically modified foods that have supporters on different sides of the fence. For example, the success of Donald Trump in 2016 represents a new paradigm in the use of social media, where unlike the use of it by Obama in 2008 and 2012 to build up a grassroots foundation to manage the "get-out-the-vote" machine, it served as a branding device to define the candidate with a very direct channel to his supporters.[28] Trump had millions of followers on Twitter, watching and listening to his every move and nuance he voiced with his tweets to explain those moves. In light of the fact that Trump was able to stitch together a wide cross-section of voters who had not supported a Republican in previous presidential runs, this represents an important example of the literature explained in this section.[29]

BRAND EXPERIENCE

Strong positive experience is another area that will become more and more important in the future, eventually leading to lower price sensitivity and increased purchases.[30] These authors explored the phenomenon of brand experience and created a typology of consumers based on their preference for brand experiences. The authors also focused on the relationship between brand attitude and purchase intentions.

According to Brakus, Schmitt, and Zarantonello, brand experience is "subjective, internal consumer responses (sensations, feelings, and cognitions) as well as behavioral responses evoked by brand-related stimuli that are part of a brand's design and identity, packaging, communications and environment."[31] Moreover, brand meaning is based on brand associations created by physical, emotional, and cognitive experiences.

The case of climate change is a perfect example of how this area of branding is becoming more important as humans witness some extreme changes in temperature around the world. In fact, 2016 has been the warmest year in the history of the world. This physical change in the planet will certainly lead to changes in the cognitive and emotional connections that people make with the subject of climate change, and the scientists and policy-makers who make arguments on both sides of the fence will have to account for the fact that there is nothing as important as a person's experience with a brand (in this case climate change) when it comes to tactical and strategic decisions on how to either reinforce or alter existing beliefs.[32]

A CALL FOR USER-GENERATED BRANDING

Yan recommended engaging in an open dialogue with brand evangelists, delivering intangible values to them, and, at the same time, avoiding commercialization, which is possible today through fostering a strong digital presence.[33] According to Yan and others, social networks and the Internet are "the next media" for the marketing of products and services, and social media engagement with customers is as important as off-line brand touch points.[34, 35]

Facebook and other social media platforms, websites, and applications are powerful tools in modern marketing. According to Yan, blogs, Facebook, and Twitter create a sense of belonging and participation.[36] Moreover, Facebook has become a commercial medium that unites not only friends but also fans and customers across the world. Last but not the least, social media transcends national borders, and streamlines international marketing activities.

Burmann recommends that companies employ powerful storytelling and narratives to engage in brand co-creation.[37] According to his research findings, user-generated messages are brand touch points that affect the consumer's brand experience and even brand expectations. He emphasized that this kind of messaging should be strategically managed to protect and strengthen brand equity. We see this frequently today in popular social media channels. Brands capitalize on the power of connectivity social media provides, and can build communities within these channels that both purposefully and organically affect consumers across the web. Like most social media channels, Facebook provides the opportunity for brands and companies to create Business Pages, where they can then connect with followers. Brands push out their content through these pages, advertising their products or services, and consumers candidly react to this content. Consumers openly voice their organic opinions, interactions, and experiences with a brand directly on the company's Business Page, and these candid opinions are accessible and readily visible to other consumers. As a result, word of mouth is incredibly powerful on social media channels, as it is easy to understand other consumers' feelings, perceptions, and experiences with the brand. Brands can gather this feedback and tailor their strategy, message, and/or products to identify what is or is not working based on consumer feedback. The real-time ability to understand and respond to consumer brand perceptions is what makes social media a powerful marketing tool for brand co-creation. The use of social media also makes it possible to more effectively create multiple meanings for brands and to direct them to different constituencies.[38]

The point is that the brand of a nation, namely Russia, was affected by the outcry of both citizens and experts alike who complained about allegations of hacking by the Russian government of democratic websites around the country. Branding can no longer be conceptualized on the basis of products and services, when it has become clear that technological advances, especially those in social media, are playing a role in the shaping attitudes and behavior of people around the world on the subjects of politics, sustainability, climate change, and other nontraditional areas. Until now, these themes had not been integrated in the branding literature from a theoretical and strategic perspective, one of the aims of this book.

BRAND PORTFOLIOS

There are several authors who have argued that top managers need to consider branding as a strategic corporate approach.[39] For example, as the role of technological change in products and media changes, and the speed at which stories can go viral, it is critical that organizations be careful about their reputation. One can look back at what happened to Hillary Clinton in the 2016 campaign when the FBI director came out only eleven days before the election and declared that there may still be a need to carry out further investigations on her alleged misuse of e-mails when she was Secretary of State. The Democratic Party as a whole was at the mercy of her reputation in the eyes of the public, and as her reputation was ultimately destroyed by the e-mail allegations, and the reputation of the Democratic Party went down along with it.

In the case of corporate brand, an individual product may in fact be the most valuable asset of a company. And unlike a political party, where elections every four years can completely alter the brand reputation of a party, as was the case in 1980, with the election of Ronald Reagan and the Republicans, or with Barack Obama and his election in 2008 and the resulting impact on the Democrats, corporation brands can suffer for a much longer time period in their attempt to re-build their reputation with a failed product or scandal, such as the BP spill, or the Carnival Cruise accident. Reputations that take years to build can be lost in just a matter of days. The real message to corporations is that they need to take very seriously their portfolio of brands, and give special attention to those brands that they may desire to use to build up brand equity, but always at a risk.[40]

According to Laforet and Saunders, there exists a significant change in brand strategies that has taken place over the past decade.[41] According to their results, there has been a reduction in the use of corporate brands, and in place of that has come the use of a combination of brand structures that they argue is necessary in more competitive markets. They point out that the goal should be shared branding strategy, where brands can share their perceived strengths and create a greater goodwill for the company. Along with this they believe will come a greater trust and awareness of the products. Their strategy for avoiding any threat to a corporate reputation is for each brand to be properly represented at the board level; keeping corporate names separate from individual brands; and to mix and match both strong and weaker together.

Paramount to the future of branding will be the realization that the best practices in branding can only come if one is able to understand how strategies change as organizations move from branding the more traditional items, like products, services, and organizations, to the branding of people, nations, and ideas. There is much to be said about the abundance of research that has been carried out in the literature to date on what works and what doesn't work in the corporate world, and to a lesser extent, in the nonprofit world, but without moving the boundaries beyond those entities, it leaves the field of branding in a vulnerable position. As the technology advances all fields, this puts the discussion of all entities in real-time, and makes the changes necessary to survive a crisis all across the increasingly influential world of social media. In the future, there will be much to be learned from the integrative knowledge that exists on branding in both the traditional and nontraditional areas.

CONCLUDING REMARKS

The ideas put forward in this book establish the role of branding in a new and innovative manner, and extends the traditional definitions and practices reported by academics and professionals over the past fifty years. The integration of the different brand entities reported in Chapters 2 through 7 bring into focus both the unique and overlapping considerations that must be accounted for when branding a product, service, person, organization, nation, or idea. The 3 C's that include the Customer, Competition, and Channel can be used to establish the strategic brand focus of whomever chooses to carry out a branding strategy, whether it is a person, corporation, nonprofit organization, or nation. Virtually anything can be branded in an effort to define and maintain a narrative one wishes to have with various publics.

Successful branding requires the choice of the right message sent through effective communication channels that enable the brand to be differentiated with the competition.

Whereas it has been established that a brand may have multiple meanings to different segments of people, it is not sufficient to get the message understood, but it must resonate in a way that establishes an emotional bond with the targeted audience. This calls for the use of tools to measure and decipher that fact that the intended meanings of the brand have been absorbed and understood so that the audience perceives the brand in the intended manner. Consequently, cultivating a thorough understanding of how the best practices reported in the book on each of the entities identified in Figure 1.1 must be brought into play.

There are a number of different branding strategies that were identified that can be used to accomplish the stated goals outlined above, and some of those that have proven to be most successful are based on the establishment of love with the brand, as well as co-branding and umbrella branding. Brand love has proven to be a highly successful strategy that helps to create strong connections to people who hold favorable perceptions of a brand, or what has been referred to as a community of strong advocates.

In order to survive in the online space, people, organizations, and even nations need to establish strong brands. Moreover, branding must be an active dialog with the consumer. To engage in a dialogue with consumers, companies need to accept the fact that they will become more vulnerable, as the digital space does not allow for harsh and unjust attitudes toward the consumer. It may only take a single mistake in the dialogue with the consumer to significantly damage the brand by creating a negative chain reaction, resulting in the defection of the brand by consumers. With the knowledge that consumers use brand names to infer the quality and value of a product sold online, it will be important to determine which information used online conveys a sense of trust and product quality with an organization's targeted audience. This is one of the greatest challenges to brand marketers who seek to compete in this retail space that do not come into it with a well-known company name and image.

As people around the world continue to rely on the Internet, branding in the digital space has created new frontiers and ways in which people and brands interact. Consumers are often dependent on the real-time and 24/7 information cycle that the Internet provides, and have come to demand real-time availability of brands. Along with this movement has come the role of the vigilante consumer who can almost instantaneously either kill or build up a brand in moments. Take the case of the elderly passenger on a United Airlines jet being violently dragged off by transportation police in Chicago. This event was recorded by a passenger, and posted throughout various social media sites. The video caught the attention of national news outlets and fueled an Internet outrage toward the United Airlines brand, leading to a PR scandal and several subsequent lawsuits that were highly publicized as well as served to further damage United's brand reputation. As a result, the company quickly announced and put into place changes in its overbooking policy to mitigate the damage to the brand. This example highlights how the world of branding is subject to new forces never before witnessed decades ago, and must be accounted for in all strategies. As evidenced by United's scandal, a brand must have an effective social media presence to respond to this kind of crisis.

Branding is a complex process that is best understood by taking into account the best practices of strategies employed by a cross-section of people and organizations in different sectors of society. The role of branding is rapidly shifting, and is becoming an increasingly more important part in all marketing strategies. The strategic brand focus presented in Figure 1.1 highlights the components that must be accounted for in all branding strategies. Whereas the targeted audience of the famous architect, Peter Marino, may be very different than the targeted audience of Vladimir Putin in Russia, each has been engaged in the successful practice of branding themselves, their ideas, as well as services through carefully chosen channels to set them apart from their competition, regardless of the fact that one is the leader of an organization and the other the leader of a nation. Although one could certainly argue that the meaning people attach to Peter Marino can range from eccentric, to biker, to successful businessman, or for Vladimir Putin, from clever political marketer, to a highly skilled politician, or to someone who is seen as a strongman in his country, each has employed the best practices reported in this book.

Ultimately, successful branding calls for utilizing the best practices that cut across the different entities covered in Chapters 2 through 7. The post-election challenge to Mr. Trump from a branding perspective is influenced by the different roles which citizens now identify with him on. Now that he is actually engaged in the role of president, his brand identity is subject to the influence of many new people, organizations, and nations in a way that it wasn't during the campaign. This very much ties into the lessons reported in this book, and attests to the fact that whereas different strategies must be used for different brand entities, it is possible that there will be overlap between them, as is the case with Mr. Trump, who needs to rely on the best practices in each of several different areas because he embodies multiple brand entities as the President of the United States. Donald Trump is a person, performing a service for the country and the world, who is seeking to drive public opinion with his ideas and strength of personality, collating personal branding, nation branding, service branding, political branding, and idea branding into a single, streamlined brand. The steps put forward in this book for successful branding represent the critical importance of understanding the fact that whereas there may be some similarities in the development and execution of branding campaigns across the categories identified in Figure 1.1, each will require very different strategies that make it possible for the brand in question to be positioned in a clear, concise manner in the minds of the targeted audience.

Endnotes

1. Wall Street Journal, 2016.
2. Diamond, 2017.
3. Kincaid, 2017.
4. Marino n.d.
5. Petersen, 2017.
6. Dalton, 2017.
7. Engeseth, 2009.
8. Yan, 2011.
9. Muñiz, Jr and Jensen Schau, Vigilante Marketing and Consumer Created Communications, 2007.
10. Gobe, 2009.
11. Muñiz, Jr and Jensen Schau, How to Inspire Value-laden Collaborative Consumer-Generated Content, 2011.
12. Antorini, Muñiz, Jr and Askildsen, 2012.
13. Yan, 2011.
14. Fournier and Avery, 2011.
15. Hatch and Schultz, 2010.
16. Berton, Pitt, Plangger, and Shapiro, 2012.
17. Craig, Sugai and Aroean, 2014.
18. Jensen Schau, Muñiz, Jr and Arnould, 2009.
19. Martini, Massa and Testa, 2014.
20. Mohanbir and Goodman, 2016.
21. O'Guinn and Muniz Jr., 2005.
22. Prahalad and Ramaswamy, 2004.
23. Hatch and Schultz, 2010.
24. Hatch and Schultz, 2010.
25. Yan, 2011.
26. Gregory, 2007.
27. Muniz and O'Guinn, 2001.
28. Newman, 2016.
29. Newman, 2016.
30. Zarantonello and Schmitt, 2010.
31. Brakus, Schmitt and Zarantonello, 2009.
32. Marino n.d.
33. Yan, 2011.
34. Yan, 2011.

35. Muñiz, Jr and Jensen Schau, How to Inspire Value-laden Collaborative Consumer-Generated Content, 2011.
36. Yan, 2011.
37. Burmann, 2010.
38. O'Guinn and Muniz Jr., 2005.
39. Laforet and Saunders, 2005.
40. Laforet and Saunders, 2005.
41. Laforet and Saunders, 2005.

BIBLIOGRAPHY

Aaker, D. A. *Building strong brands.* New York: The Free Press, 1996.

Aaker, D. A., and Jacobson, R. 1994. "The financial information content of perceived quality." *Journal of Marketing Research,* 191–201.

Aaker, D. A. "The Five Biggest Ideas of the Branding Era." *Marketing Management,* 2014: 22–23.

Adobe. n.d. *Marketing has changed more in the past two years than in the past 50.* Accessed February 2017. https://qz.com/132776/marketing-has-changed-more-in-the-past-two-years-than-in-the-past-50/.

Alani, F. *Did social media change the 2010 general election?* May 2010. http://www.computerweekly.com/feature/Did-social-media-change-the-2010-General-Election.

Anholt, S. "Anholt Nation Brands Index: How Does the World See America?" *Journal of Advertising Research,* 2005: 296–304.

Anholt, S., and J. Hildreth. *Brand America: The Mother of all Brands.* London: Cyan Books, 2004.

Antorini, Y. M., A. M. Muñiz, Jr., and T. Askildsen. "Collaborating with User Innovation Communities: Lessons from the LEGO Group." *MIT Sloan Management Review* 53 (2012).

Arruda, W. *Why LinkedIn Is The Only Personal Branding Resource You Need.* June 10, 2014. http://www.forbes.com/sites/williamarruda/2014/06/10/why-linkedin-is-the-only-personal-branding-resource-you-need/.

Arslan, F. M., and O. K. Altuna. 2010. "The effect of brand extensions on product brand image." *Journal of Product & Brand Management,* 170–180. doi:10.1108/10610421011046157.

Asmus, P. *The case against Chevron.* December 2009. http://www.eastbayexpress.com/oakland/the-case-against-chevron/Content?oid=1514228.

Azoulay, A, and J Kapferer. 2003. "Do brand personality scales really measure brand personality?" *Journal Of Brand Management,* 143–155.

Baghi, I., and V. Gabrielli. "For-profit or non-profit brands: Which are more effective in a cause-related marketing programme?" *Journal of Brand Management,* April 2012: 218–231.

Baker, G. A., and T. A. Burnham. "Consumer response to genetically modified foods: market segment analysis and implications for producers and policy makers." *Journal of Agricultural and Resource Economics,* 2001: 387–403.

Ballantyne, D., and R. Aitken. "Branding in B2B markets: insights from the service-dominant logic of marketing." *Journal of Business & Industrial Marketing,* 2007: 363–371.

Balmer, J. M. "Corporate identity, corporate branding and corporate marketing-seeing through the fog." *European journal of marketing,* 2001: 248–291.

Balmer, J. M., and S. A. Greyser. "Corporate marketing: Integrating corporate identity, corporate branding, corporate communications, corporate image and corporate reputation." *European Journal of Marketing*, 2006: 730–741.

Bandura, A. *Social foundations of thought and action: A social cognitive theory.* Englewood Cliffs, NJ: Prentice-Hall, 1986.

Batra, R., A. Ahuvia, and R. P. Bagozzi. "Brand love." *Journal of Marketing* 76, no. 2 (2012): 1–16.

Beckwith, N. E., and D. R. Lehmann. 1975. "The importance of halo effects in multi-attribute attitude model." *Journal Of Marketing Research*, 265–275.

Behr, A., and A. Beeler-Norrholm. "Fame, fortune, and the occasional branding misstep: When good celebrities go bad." *Intellectual Property & Technology Law Journal*, 2006: 6–11.

Belk, R. W. "Possessions and the extended self." *Journal of Consumer Research 15(2)*, 1988: 139–168.

Bendisch, F., G. Larsen, and M. Trueman. *Branding people: towards a conceptual framework.* Bradford University of Management, 2007.

Bergkvist, L., and T. Bech-Larsen. "Two studies of consequences and actionable antecedents of brand love." *Journal of Brand Management, 17(7)*, 2010: 504–518. doi:10.1057/bm.2010.6.

Berry, L. "Big ideas in services marketing." *Journal of Consumer Marketing*, 1986: 47–51.

Berry, L. L. "Cultivating service brand equity." *Journal of the Academy of Marketing Science*, 2000: 128–137.

Berry, L. L., E. F. Lefkowith, and T. Clark. "In services, what's in a name." *Harvard Business Review*, 1988: 28–30.

Berthon, P., L. Pitt, K. Plangger, and D. Shapiro. "Marketing Meets Web 2.0, Social Media, and Creative Consumers: Implications for International Marketing Strategy." *Business Horizons*, 2012: 261–271.

Berthon, P., M. B. Holbrook, J. M. Hulbert, and L. Pitt. "Viewing brands in multiple dimensions." *MIT Sloan Management Review*, 2007: 37.

Besharat, A., and R. Langan. "Towards the formation of consensus in the domain of co-branding: current findings and future priorities." *Journal of Brand Management, 21(2)*, 2013: 112–132.

Bissell, K., and A. Rask. "Real women on real beauty: Self-discrepancy, internalization of the thin ideal, and perceptions of attractiveness and thinness in Dove's Campaign for Real Beauty." *International Journal of Advertising*, 2010: 29.

Booms, B. H., and M. J. Bitner. "Marketing strategies and organization structures for service firms." *Marketing of services*, 1981: 47–52.

Brakus, J. J., B. H. Schmitt, and L. Zarantonello. "Brand experience: What is it? How is it measured? Does it affect loyalty?" *Journal of marketing, 73(3)*, 2009: 52–68.

Bredahl, L. "Consumers cognitions with regard to genetically modified foods. Results of a qualitative study in four countries." *Appetite*, 1999: 343–360.

Brennan, J., and L. Mattice. "The importance of personal branding." *City Security Magazine*, 2014: 93.

Brescoll, V. L., E. L. Uhlmann, and G. E. Newman. "The effects of system-justifying motivations on endorsement of essentialist explanations for gender differences." *Journal of Personality and Social Psychology*, 2013: 891–908.

Brescoll, V. L., and E. L. Uhlmann. "Can an angry woman get ahead? Gender, status conferral, and workplace emotion expression." *Psychological Science*, 2008: 268–275.

Burmann, C. "A call for 'User-Generated Branding." *Journal Of Brand Management, 18(1)*, 2010: 1–4.

Calder, R., and Cook. "What it takes to be an irresistible brand." *Warc.com.* May 2014.

Carroll, B. A., and A. C. Ahuvia. "Some antecedents and outcomes of brand love." *Marketing letters* 17, no. 2 (2006): 79–89.

Chaney, S. "Web Retailer Nasty Gal Has Not-So-Nice Ending." *Wall Street Journal*, February 2017: B4.

Charlene, D. J. "A conceptual view of branding for services." *Innovative Marketing*, 2007: 7–14.

Charry, K. "Product placement and the promotion of healthy food to preadolescents: When popular TV series make carrots look cool." *International Journal of Advertising*, 2014: 33.

Chou, H., and N. Lien. "How do candidate poll ranking and election status affect the effects of negative political advertising?" *International Journal of Advertising* 29, no. 5 (2010).

Cieslak, J. *What We Can Learn from Uber's Logo Debacle.* February 4, 2016.

"ComRes and the Grantham Institute on Climate Change and the Environment: Increasing digital influence over the climate change debate." *MRS AwardsWinner.* December 2014.

Cone Communications. n.d. "The 2013 Cone Communications Social Impact Study." http://www.conecomm.com/2013-social-impact-release.

Coulter, K. "The Tri-Mediation Model of persuasion: a case for negative political advertising?" *International Journal of Advertising* 27, no. 5 (2008).

Craig, T., P. Sugai, and L. Aroean. "Hatsune Miku: Japanese Virtual Idol Ignites Global Value Co-creation." Ivey School of Business, 2014.

Dall'Olmo, R. F., and L. de Chernatony. "The Service Brand as Relationships Builder." *British Journal of Management*, 2000: 137–150.

Dalton, M. "The Stores that Cater to the 0.1%, not the 1%." *Wall Street Journal*, March 16, 2017: A17, A19.

Davis, J. C. "A conceptual view of branding for services." *Innovative marketing*, 2007: 7.

Davis, R., M. Buchanan-Oliver, and R. J. Brodie. "Retail Service Branding in Electronic-Commerce Environments." *Journal of Service Research*, 2000: 178.

de Bakker, F. G., P. Groenewegen, and F. Den Hond. "A bibliometric analysis of 30 years of research and theory on corporate social responsibility and corporate social performance." *Business & Society*, 2005: 283–317.

de Bussy, N. M., M. T. Ewing, P. Berthon, and L. Pitt. "Employment Branding In The Knowledge Economy." *International Journal of Advertising* 21, no. 1 (2002).

de Chernatony, L. "Brand management through narrowing the gap between brand identity and brand reputation." *Journal of Marketing Management*, 1999: 157–179.

de Chernatony, L., and F. D. Riley. "Experts' views about defining services brands and the principles of services branding." *Journal of Business Research*, 1999: 181–192.

de Chernatony, L, and S. Segal-Horn. "Building on services' characteristics to develop successful services brands." *Journal of Marketing Management*, 2001: 645–669.

Detsiny, M. "The obesity crisis: how should the food and soft drinks industry react?" *Market Leader*, 2004: 25.

Diamond, J. "How Gonzaga Became a Top Dog." *Wall Street Journal*, April 3, 2017: A18.

Dickinson, S., and A. Barker. "Evaluations of branding alliances between non-profit and commercial brand partners: the transfer of affect." *International Journal of Nonprofit and Voluntary Sector Marketing*, 2007: 75–89.

Dinnie, K., T. C. Melewar, K. U. Seidenfuss, and G. Musa. "Nation branding and integrated marketing communications: an ASEAN perspective." *International Marketing Review*, 2010: 388–403.

Dou, W., and S. Krishnamurthy. "Using brand websites to build brands online: a product versus service brand comparison." *Journal of Advertising Research*, June 2007: 1–19, 193–206.

Edwards, S. M., and C. La Ferle. "Does Gender Impact the Perception of Negative Information Related to Celebrity Endorsements?" *Journal of Promotion Management*, 2009: 22–35.

Einwiller, S., and M. Will. "Towards an integrated approach to corporate branding—An empirical study." *Corporate Communications*, 2002: 100–109.

Engeseth, S. *The Fall of PR and the Rise of Advertising*. Stockholm: Stefan Engeseth Publishing, 2009.

Environmental Defense Fund. *Our Mission and Values*. 2017.

Evans, W. D., J. Blitstein, J. C. Hersey, J. Renaud, and A. L. Yaroch. "Systematic review of public health branding." *Journal of Health Communication*, 2008: 721–741.

Fan, Y. "Branding the nation: Towards a better understanding." *Place Branding & Public Diplomacy*, 2010: 97–103.

Fan, Y. "Ethical branding and corporate reputation." *Corporate Communications*, 2005: 341–350.

Fischer, M. n.d. *Valuing brand assets: a cost-effective and easy-to-implement measurement approach*. MSI Reports: Working Papers Series, Cambridge: Marketing Science Institute, 7–107.

Fisk, R. P., S. W. Brown, and M. J. Bitner. "Tracking the evolution of the services marketing literature." *Journal of Retailing*, 1993: 61–103.

Ford Motor Company. *Our Vision*. 2017.

Fournier, S. "Consumers and their brands: Developing relationship theory in consumer research." *Journal of Consumer Research*, 1998: 343–373.

Fournier, S., and J. Avery. "The Uninvited Brand." *Business Horizons*, 2011: 193–207.

Fournier, S. "Exploring Brand-Person Relationships: Three Life Histories." *Harvard Business Review*. 1997.

Fournier, S., J. Quelch, and B. Reitveld. "To Get More out of Social Media, Think Like an Anthropologist." *Harvard Business Review*, 2016.

Fournier, S., M. Solomon, and B. G. Englis. "When brands resonate." *Handbook of brand and experience management*, 2008: 35–57.

Francis, K. "The rise of the connected consumer demands trust." *Marque*. October 10, 2011. http://marque.co.nz/archive/rise-of-the-connected-consumer (accessed January 2, 2012).

French, A., and G. Smith. "Measuring political brand equity: a consumer oriented approach." *European Journal of Marketing*, 2010: 460–477.

Friestad, M., and P. Wright. "The persuasion knowledge model: how people cope with persuasion attempts." *Journal of Consumer Research*, 1994: 1–31.

Funk, C., and L Raine. "Americans, politics and science issues." *Pew Research Center*. 2016. http://www.pewinternet.org/2015/07/01/chapter-6-public-opinion-about-food/.

Gallup. "Worry about terror attacks in U.S. high, but not top concern." *Gallup*. 2016. http://www.gallup.com/poll/190253/worry-terror-attacks-high-not-top-concern.aspx?g_source=Politics&g_medium=lead&g_campaign=tiles.

Garbacz-Rawson, E. A. "Perceptions of the United States of America: Exploring the political brand of a nation." *Place Branding and Public Diplomacy*, 2007: 213–221.

Gasparro, A. "Spicing Up American Food Brands." *Wall Street Journal*, May 2017: B13.

George, W. R., and L. L. Berry. "Guidelines for the advertising of services." *Business Horizons*, 1981: 52–56.

Gianatasio, D. "Tapping Millennial Political and Social Passions Ahead of the Midterm Elections. These agencies specialize in Gen Y." *Adweek*. October 6, 2014.

Gobe, M. *Emotional branding*. Allworth Press, 2009.

Gobe, M. *Emotional branding: the new paradigm for connecting brands to people*. Allworth Press, 2001.

Grace, D., and A. O'Cass. "Service branding: Consumer verdicts on service brands." *Journal of Retailing & Consumer Services*, 2005: 125–139.

Greenpeace. *Our Core Values*. 2017.

Gregory, A. "Involving stakeholders in developing corporate brands: The communication dimension." *Journal of Marketing Management*, 2007: 59–73.

Gyrd-Jones, R. I., and N. Kornum. "Managing the co-created brand: Value and cultural complementarity in online and offline multi-stakeholder ecosystems." *Journal of Business Research*, 2013: 1484–1493.

Hagenbuch, D. *3 Infallible Principles for Personal Branding From Pope Francis*. October 5, 2016. https://www.entrepreneur.com/article/251326.

Hamann, D., R. Williams, and M. Omar. "Branding strategy and consumer high-technology product." *Journal of Product & Brand Management*, 2007: 98–111.

Hamlin, R. P., and T. Wilson. "The impact of cause branding on consumer reactions to products: does product/cause 'fit' really matter?" *Journal of Marketing Management*, 2004: 20(7–8), 663–681.

Han, C. M., and V. Terpstra. "Country-of-origin effects for uni-national and bi-national products." *Journal Of International Business Studies*, 1988: 235–255.

Harris, F., and L. de Chernatony. "Corporate branding and corporate brand performance." *European Journal of marketing*, 2001: 441–456.

Hatch, M. J., and M. Schultz. "Bringing the corporation into corporate branding." *European Journal of Marketing*, 2003: 1041–64.

Hatch, M. J., and M. Schultz. "Toward a theory of brand co-creation with implications for brand governance." *Journal of Brand Management*, 2010: 590–604.

Hendawi, H. "He mixes 'authoritarianism and PR." *Wall Street Journal*, May 2017: 29.

Heslop, L. A., J. Nadeau, N. O'Reilly, and A. Armenakyan. "Mega-event and country co-branding: Image shifts, transfers and reputational impacts." *Corporate Reputation Review*, 2013: 7–33.

Hicks, C. D. "The future of sustainability-driven partnerships and a new role for brand strategy." *Journal of Brand Management*, 2013: 255–262.

Hirschman, E. C. "Evolutionary Branding." *Psychology and Marketing*, 2010: 568–583.

Hoegg, J., and M. Lewis. "The impact of candidate appearance and advertising strategies on election results." *Journal Of Marketing Research*, 2011: 895–909.

Hogl, S., and O. Hupp. *Managing corporate brands successfully—approaches for strategic corporate communications.* Cannes, September 2005.

Hollis, N. *Branding in the service economy.* January 2014.

Holt, D. B. 2002. "Why do brands cause trouble? A dialectical theory of consumer culture and branding." *Journal of Consumer Research* 70–90.

Holt, D. B. *How brands become icons: The principles of cultural branding.* Harvard Business Press, 2004.

Holt, D. B. "What becomes an icon most?" *Harvard Business Review*, 2003: 43–49.

Horton, D., and R. Wohl. "Mass communication and para-social interaction: Observations on intimacy at a distance." *Psychiatry: Journal for the Study of Interpersonal Processes*, 1956: 215–229.

Ilicic, J., and C. M. Webster. "Effects of multiple endorsements and consumer–celebrity attachment on attitude and purchase intention." *Australasian Marketing Journal*, 2011: 230–237.

Innes, J. M., and H. Zeitz. "The public's view of the impact of the mass media: A test of the 'third person' effect." *European Journal of Social Psychology*, 1988: 457–463.

Jacoby, J., and J. C. Olson. 1970. *An attitude model of brand loyalty: Conceptual underpinnings and instrumentation research.* New York: John Wiley & Sons.

Jansen, S. C. "Designer nations: Neo-liberal nation branding–Brand Estonia." *Social identities*, 2008: 121–142.

Jensen Schau, H., A. M. Muñiz, Jr., and E. J. Arnould. "How Brand Community Practices Create Value." *Journal of Marketing* 73 (September 2009): 30–51.

Jung, C. G. *The Archetypes and the Collective Unconscious.* Princeton: Bollingen, 1938.

Kaplan, A. M., and M. Haenlein. "Users of the world, unite! The challenges and opportunities of Social Media." *Business horizons*, 2010: 59–68.

Keller, K. L. 2003. "Brand synthesis: the multidimensionality of consumer knowledge." *Journal of Consumer Research,* 595–600.

Keller, K. L., and D. R. Lehmann. 2006. "Brands and branding: Research findings and future priorities." *Marketing science*, 740–759.

Keränen, J., K.A. Piirainen, and R. T. Salminen. "Systematic review on B2B branding: research issues and avenues for future research." *Journal of Product & Brand Management* 21, no. 6 (2012): 404–417.

Kim, Y. K., S. W. Shim, and K. Dinnie. "The dimensions of nation brand personality: A study of nine countries." *Corporate Reputation Review*, 2013: 34–47.

Kincaid, E. "Emoji Beckon As 'Gold Mine' for Marketers." *Wall Street Journal*, April 7, 2017: B4.

Kitchen, P. J., J. Brignell, T. Li, and G. S. Jones. "The emergence of IMC: a theoretical perspective." *Journal of Advertising Research*, 2004: 19–30.

Kotler, P., and G. Armstrong. *Principles of marketing.* Upper Saddle River, NJ: Prentice Hall, 2010.

Kotler, P., and G. Zaltman. "Social marketing: an approach to planned social change." *The Journal of Marketing*, 1971: 3–12.

Kowalczyk, C. M., and M. B. Royne. "The Moderating Role of Celebrity Worship on Attitudes Toward Celebrity Brand Extensions." *Journal Of Marketing Theory & Practice*, 2013: 211–220.

Laforet, S., and J. Saunders. "Managing Brand Portfolios: How Strategies Have Changed." *Journal of Advertising Research*, 2005: Vol. 45, No. 3.

Lair, D., K. Sullivan, and G. Cheney. "Marketization and the recasting of the professional self: the rhetoric and ethics of personal branding." *Management Communication Quarterly*, 307–343.

Lapowsky, I. "4 takeaways from the iconic 'Got Milk?' ad campaign." *Inc.* February 24, 2014. http://www.inc.com/issie-lapowsky/marketing-tips-got-milk.html.

Leclerc, F., B. H. Schmitt, and L. Dubé. "Foreign branding and its effects on product perceptions and attitudes." *Journal of Marketing Research*, 1994: 263–270.

Leigh, A., and T. Susilo. "Is voting skin-deep? Estimating the effect of candidate ballot photographs on election outcomes." *Journal of Economic Psychology* 30, no. 1 (2009): 61–70.

Leuthesser, L., C. Kohli, and R. Suri. "2+2 =5? A framework for using co-branding to leverage a brand." *Journal of Brand Management*, 2003: 35–47.

Lin, L. 2010. "The relationship of consumer personality trait, brand personality and brand loyalty: an empirical study of toys and video games buyers." *Journal of Product & Brand Management*, 4–17. doi:10.1108/10610421011018347.

Louis, D., and C. Lombart. 2010. "Impact of brand personality on three major relational consequences (trust, attachment, and commitment to the brand)." *Journal of Product & Brand Management*, 114–130. doi:10.1108/10610421011033467.

Lovelock, C. H., and L. Wright. *Principles of service marketing and management.* Upper Saddle River, N.J: Prentice Hall, 1999.

Mainwaring, S. 2013. *Marketing 3.0: The rise of purpose-driven social brands [infographic].* http://wefirstbranding.com/purpose/marketing-3-0-the-rise-of-purpose-driven-social-brands-infographic/

Maloney, J. "Coca-Cola Needs to Be More Than Just Coke, Its Next Chief Says." *Wall Street Journal*, February 2017: B3.

Maloney, J. "Shaking the 'New Coke Syndrome.'" *Wall Street Journal*, May 2017: B1–B2.

Marshall, J., and R. Wise. "The Resurgence of the Corporate Brand." *Advertising Age.* 2013. http://adage.com/article/cmo-strategy/resurgence-corporate-brand/240855/. (accessed September 12, 2014).

Martinez, E., and L. de Chernatony. 2004. "The effect of brand extension strategies upon brand image." *Journal of consumer marketing,* 39–50.

Martini, A., S. Massa, and S. Testa. "Customer Co-creation Projects and Social Media: The Case of Barilla of Italy." *Business Horizons*, 2014: 425–434.

Matthews, C. *Republicans suspend February NBC debate: Here's why.* October 30, 2015. http://fortune.com/2015/10/30/nbc-republican-cnbc-debate/.

Mattila, A. "The Role of Narratives in the Advertising of Services." *Journal of Services Research*, 2000: 35–45.

McCracken, G. "Who is the celebrity endorser? Cultural foundations of the endorsement process." *Journal of Consumer Research*, 1989: 310–321.

McCright, A. M., and R. E. Dunlap. "The politicization of climate change and polarization in the American public's views of global warming, 2001–2010." *Sociological Quarterly*, 2011: 155–194.

McCutcheon, L., and H. Lange. "Conceptualization and Measurement of Celebrity Worship." *British Journal of Psychology*, 2002: 68–87.

Melnik, M. I., and J. Alm. 2002. "Does a seller's ecommerce reputation matter? Evidence from eBay auctions." *The Journal of Industrial Economics*, 337–349.

Miller, T. "'Got Milk' ad campaign retired after 20 years of milk moustaches." *Daily News.* February 25, 2014. http://www.nydailynews.com/life-style/health/milk-ads-retired-20-years-milk-moustaches-article-1.1701064.

Mohanbir, S., and P. Goodman. "The Hunger Games: Catching Fire: Using Digital and Social Media for Brand Storytelling." Kellogg, 2016.

Moilanen, T., and S. Rainisto. *How to brand nations, cities and destinations: a planning book for place branding.* Palgrave Macmillan, 2008.

Moorman, C. *The Riddle of Marketing in Russia.* February 18, 2014. http://www.forbes.com/sites/christinemoorman/2014/02/18/the-riddle-of-marketing-in-russia/#5a0081276019.

Mudambi, S. M., P. Doyle, and V. Wong. "An exploration of branding in industrial markets." *Industrial Marketing Management*, 1997: 433–446.

Muniz, A. M., and T. C. O'Guinn. "Brand community." *Journal of Consumer Research*, 2001: 412–432.

Muñiz, Jr., A. M., and H. Jensen Schau. "How to Inspire Value-laden Collaborative Consumer-Generated Content." *Business Horizons*, 2011: 209–217.

Muñiz, Jr., A. M., and Hope Jensen Schau. "Vigilante Marketing and Consumer Created Communications." *Journal of Advertising* 36 (2007): 35–50.

Muñiz Jr., A. M. "Brands and Branding." In *Encyclopedia of Sociology, 2nd Edition*, by George Ritzer and Wiley Blackwell. 2015.

Newman, B. I. "Reinforcing Lessons for Business from the Marketing Revolution in U.S. Presidential Politics: A Strategic Triad." *Psychology & Marketing* 33, no. 10 (2016): 781–795.

Newman, B. I. "Editorial: Broadening the boundaries of marketing: Political marketing in the new millennium." *Psychology & Marketing* 9, no. 12 (2002): 983–986.

Newman, B. I. *The Handbook of Political Marketing.* California: Sage Publications, 1999.

Newman, B. I. *The Marketing of the President.* California: Sage Publications, 1994.

Newman, B. I. *The Marketing Revolution in Politics: What Recent U.S. Presidential Campaigns Can Teach Us About Effective Marketing.* Toronto: Rotman-UTP, 2016.

Newman, C. L., E. Howlett, S. Burton, J. C. Kozup, and T. Heintz. "The influence of consumer concern about global climate change on framing effects for environmental sustainability messages." *International Journal of Advertising*, 2012: 3.

Newman, G. E., M. Gorlin, and R. Dhar. "When going green backfires: How firm intentions shape the evaluation of socially beneficial product enhancements." *Journal of Consumer Research*, 2014: 823–839.

Nightingale, T. *Marketing from a political perspective*. 2012. http://adage.com/article/btob/marketing-a-political-perspective/286950/.

Nisbet, M. C. *Public opinion and participation*. Edited by J. S. Dryzek and R. B. Norgaard. Oxford: Oxford University Press, 2011.

Nisbet, M. C., and T. P. Newman. "Framing, the Media, and Environmental Communication." In *The Routledge Handbook of Environment and Communication*, by H. Anders and R. Cox, 325–338. London: Routledge, 2015.

Nye Jr., J. S. *Soft Power: The Means to Success in World Politics*. Cambridge: Perseus Books Group, 2004.

O'Cass, A., and R. Voola. "Explications of political market orientation and political brand orientation using the resource-based view of the political party." *Journal of Marketing Management*, 2011: 627.

O'Guinn, T. C., and A. M. Muniz Jr. "13 Communal consumption and the brand." *Inside consumption: Consumer motives, goals, and desires*, 2005: 252.

O'Guinn, T. C., and A. M. Muñiz Jr. "Towards a Sociological Model of Brands." In *Brands and Brand Management: Contemporary Research Perspectives*, by Barbara Loken, Ahluwalia Rohini and Michael J Houston. New York: Taylor and Francis, 2010.

Papadopoulos, N., and L. Heslop. "Country equity and country branding: Problems and prospects." *The Journal of Brand Management*, 2002: 294–314.

Papadopoulos, N., and L. A. Heslop. "Product-country images: Impact and role in international marketing." *Routledge*, 2014.

Park, C. W., B. J. Jaworski, and D. J. MacInnis. "Strategic brand concept-image management." *The Journal of Marketing*, 1986: 135–145.

Perloff, R. M. *The dynamics of political communication: Media and politics in a digital age*. 2. New York: Routledge, 2018.

"Peter Marino." *Wikipedia*.

Petersen, A. "How Hotel Companies Launch New Brands." *Wall Street Journal*, January 3, 2017: A11.

Phillipson, I. *Married to the job: Why we live to work and what we do about it*. New York: Free Press, 2002.

Phipps, M., J. Brace-Govan, and C. Jevons. "The duality of political brand equity." *European Journal of Marketing*, 2010: 496–514.

Porter, M. E., and M. R. Kramer. "Strategy and society." *Harvard business review*, 2006: 78–92.

Prahalad, C. K., and V. Ramaswamy. *The future of competition: co-creating unique value with customers*. Boston: Harvard Business School Press, 2004.

Precourt, G. "TOMS Shoes: Five basic best practices for purpose-driven marketing." *ANA Digital & Social Media.* July 2014. www.warc.com/precourt.

Pringle, H., and L. Binet. "How marketers can use celebrities to sell more effectively." *Journal of Consumer Behavior*, 2005: 201–214.

Radighieri, J. P., J. Mariadoss, Y. Grégoire, and J. Johnson. "Ingredient branding and feedback effects: The impact of product outcomes, initial parent brand strength asymmetry, and parent brand role." Marketing Letters, 25(2), 123–138. 2014.

Rampersad, H. "Step by step to an authentic personal brand." *Training & Management Development Methods*, 2010: 401–406.

Randle, M., F. Leisch, and S. Dolnicar. "Competition or collaboration? The effect of non-profit brand image on volunteer recruitment strategy." *Journal of Brand Management*, 2013: 689–704.

Rao, V. R., M. K. Agarwal, and D. Dahlhoff. "How is manifest branding strategy related to the intangible value of a corporation?" *Journal of Marketing*, 2004: 126–141.

Reeves, P., L. de Chernatony, and M. Carrigan. "Building a political brand: Ideology or voter-driven strategy." *The Journal of Brand Management*, 2006: 418–428.

Reid, D., P. Baird, A. J. Bailie, and D. Lyle. "Anti-Drink Driving—'Shame' Campaign." *Institute of Practitioners in Advertising Silver Medal, IPA Effectiveness Awards 2002.* Warc.com. 2002.

Ries, A., and L. Ries. 2009. *The 22 immutable laws of branding.* Harper Collins.

Roll, M. "Understanding the purpose of a corporate branding strategy." *BrandChannel.* 2004.

Romero, J., and M. J. Yagüe. 2015. "Relating brand equity and customer equity." *International Journal of Market Research* 631–651. doi:10.2501.

Rooney, A. "Branding: a trend for today and tomorrow." *Journal Of Product & Brand Management*, 1995: 45–55.

Rummel, J. "Catholic Archdiocese of New York: The New York Priest. God knows what He does for a living campaign." *Encyclopedia of Major Marketing Campaigns*, 2000: 1.

Scammell, M. "Political marketing: Lessons for political science." *Political Studies*, 1999: 718–739.

Schultz, M., and M. Hatch. "The cycles of corporate branding: the case of the Lego company." *California Management Review*, 2003: 6–26.

Seno, D., and B. A. Lukas. 2007. "The equity effect of product endorsement by celebrities: A conceptual framework from a co-branding perspective." *European Journal of Marketing*, 121–134.

Shankar, V., P. Azar, and M. Fuller. 2008. "BRAND'EQT: A multicategory brand equity model and its application at Allstate." *Marketing Science*, 567–584.

Shocker, A. D., and B. Weitz. 1988. "A perspective on brand equity principles and issues." *Defining, Measuring, and Managing Brand Equity: Conf. Summary.* Cambridge, MA: Marketing Science Institute. Rep. No. 88-104.

Singer, C. "Bringing brand savvy to politics." *Brandweek*, September 2002: 19.

Solomon, M. *Consumer behavior: buying, having and being.* Upper Saddle River, NJ: Pearson Education/Prentice Hall, 2009.

Solomon, M. *Your Customer Service Style is You Brand: The Ritz Carlon Case Study.* September 24, 2015.

STAFF, ENTREPRENEUR. *SMALL BUSINESS ENCYCLOPEDIA.* https://www.entrepreneur.com/encyclopedia/branding.

Starbucks Corporation. *Tackling Climate Change.* 2017.

Sternberg, R. J. "Liking versus loving: A comparative evaluation of theories." *Psychological Bulletin,* 1987: 331–345.

Stride, H., and S. Lee. "No logo? No way. Branding in the non-profit sector." *Journal of Marketing Management,* 2007: 107–122.

Szondi, G. "The role and challenges of country branding in transition countries: The Central and Eastern European experience." *Place Branding and Public Diplomacy,* 2007: 8–20.

Thompson, C. J., A. Rindfleisch, and Z. Arsel. "Emotional branding and the strategic value of the doppelgänger brand image." *Journal of Marketing,* 2006: 50–64.

Thomson, M. "Human Brands: Investigating Antecedents to Consumers' Strong Attachments to Celebrities." *Journal of Marketing,* 2006: 104–119.

Tsai, S. "Investigating archetype-icon transformation in brand marketing." *Marketing Intelligence & Planning,* 2006: 648–663.

Tumulty, K., P. Rucker, and R. Costa. *GOP leaders fear damage to party's image as Donald Trump doubles down.* July 8, 2015. https://www.washingtonpost.com/politics/trump-could-damage-the-republican-image-party-leaders-worry/2015/07/08/2ec75b4c-25ab-11e5-b72c-2b7d516e1e0e_story.html?utm_term=.a4e550ad8908.

Twitchell, J. "An English Teacher Looks at Branding." *Journal of Consumer Research,* 2004: 484–489.

Tyrrell, B, and T. Westall. "The new service ethos, a post-brand future—and how to avoid it." *Market Leader,* 1998: 14–19.

Udell, M. 2014. *What's in a Brand?* https://www.ama.org/publications/MarketingInsights/Pages/whats-in-a-brand.aspx.

Um, N. "Effects of Negative Brand Information: Measuring Impact of Celebrity Identification and Brand Commitment." *Journal Of Global Marketing,* 2013: 68–79.

Urde, M. "Core value-based corporate brand building." *European Journal of Marketing,* 2003: 1017–1040.

Vargas, J. "Brands to take the initiative in Mexican battle with obesity." *TNS: Intelligence Applied,* October 2014.

Vargo, S. L., and R. F. Lusch. "Evolving to a new dominant logic for marketing." *Journal of Marketing,* 2004: 1–17.

Voeth, M., and U. Herbst. "The concept of brand personality as an instrument for advanced non-profit branding–An empirical analysis." *Journal of Nonprofit & Public Sector Marketing,* 2008: 71–97.

Wall Street Journal. December 23, 2016. A1, A9.

"Warc briefing: Service brands." *Warc Exclusive.* November 2010.

Ward, M. R., and M. J. Lee. "Internet shopping, consumer search and product branding." *Journal of product & brand management,* 2000: 6–20.

Wernerfelt, B. "Umbrella branding as a signal of new product quality: an example of signaling by posting a bond." *The Rand Journal of Economics*, 1988: 458–466.

Whiteside, S. "Creating a More Human Brand Image: McDonald's Social Media Strategy." *Event Reports, Warc Corporate Social Media*. 2013.

Whitmarsh, L. "What's in a name? Commonalities and differences in public understanding of 'climate change' and 'global warming.'" *Public Understanding of Science*, 2009: 401–420.

Wilner, E. *Toothpaste vs. Candidates: Why the mad men approach doesn't work in politics*. 2012. http://adage.com/article/campaign-trail/toothpaste-candidates-ads/236643/.

Wood, J. "Does negative and comparative advertising work." *Admap*, January 2003.

Wright, B. "Brand meaning: In search of brand magic." *Warc.om*. March 2014.

Wright, C. *Why GOP brand is broken*. November 13, 2015. http://www.cnn.com/2015/11/13/opinions/wright-republican-presidential-field/,November.

Yan, J. "Social media in branding: Fulfilling a need." *Journal of Brand Management*, 2011: 688–696.

Zarantonello, L., and B. H. Schmitt. "Using the brand experience scale to profile consumers and predict consumer behaviour." *Journal of Brand Management*, 2010: 532–540.

Zuckerberg, M. *Oculus VR Purchase Announcement*. 2016.

NAME INDEX

A

Aaker, D. A., 18, 35, 87, 127
Abdel-Fettah el-Sissi, 128–129
Abercrombie & Fitch, 143
Airbnb, 56, 75
Aitken, R., 45
Alani, F., 71
Alm, J., 34
Altuna, O. K., 29
American Medical Association (AMA), 135
Amoruso, Sophia, 36
Apple Corporation, 10, 11, 15, 64
Armenakyan, A., 114
Armstrong, G., 18
Arslan, F. M., 29
Azoulay, A., 31

B

Baghi, I., 92, 93
Bailie, A. J., 132
Baird, P., 132
Ballantyne, D., 45
Balmer, J. M., 83, 86
Bandura, Albert, 70, 77
Bech-Larsen, T., 17
Beckwith, N. E., 35
Beeler-Norrholm, A., 68
Behr, A., 68
Belk, R. W., 16, 17

Ben & Jerry's, 28
Bergkvist, L., 17
Berry, L. L., 44, 49, 60
Berthon, P., 89
Besharat, A., 18, 19
Beyoncé, 34
Binet, L., 67
Bissell, K., 133
Bitner, M. J., 43, 45
BMW, 20, 81
Boohoo.com, 36
Booms, B. H., 45
BP, 89, 164
Brace-Govan, J., 95, 98
Brady, Tom, 64
Brakus, J. J., 162
Brennan, J., 65
Brescoll, V. L., 65
Brodie, R. J., 50
Brown, S. W., 43
Buchanan-Oliver, M., 50
Burmann, C., 163
Burton, S., 133
Bush, George W., 55

C

Calder, R., 15, 16
Callahan, Emily, 94
Carnival Cruise Line, 46, 122, 164
Carrigan, M., 70, 95

SUBJECT INDEX

CPSIA information can be obtained
at www.ICGtesting.com
Printed in the USA
LVHW020819061218
599141LV00001B/1/P

9 781524 959456